# THE RESURRECTION CODE

Books on John's gospel by the author:

*John's Gospel, New Testament Readings* (London/New York: Routledge, 1994)

*The Gospel of John as Literature: An Anthology of Twentieth Century Perspectives* (Leiden: E.J. Brill Publishers, 1993)

*John. Readings: A New Biblical Commentary* (Sheffield: JSOT Press, 1993)

*John as Storyteller. Narrative Criticism and the Fourth Gospel* (Cambridge: Cambridge University Press, 1992)

# The Resurrection Code
## Mary Magdalene
## and the Easter Enigma

Mark Stibbe

Authentic

MILTON KEYNES ● COLORADO SPRINGS ● HYDERABAD

*This book is dedicated to my mother,
Joy Stibbe, with deep gratitude for adopting me,
and for all love shown through five decades.*

# Contents

# Acknowledgements

I would like to express my heartfelt thanks to Dwight Pryor not only for the wonderful foreword he has written for *The Resurrection Code*, but also for his insightful appendix on the actual time when Jesus rose from the dead. Dwight's Hebraic understanding of the Scriptures has led him to believe that Jesus rose from the dead on Saturday evening, not Sunday morning. This is the clear implication of a Hebraic reading of John 20:1, where we read that Mary Magdalene came to the tomb of Jesus very early on the first day of the week. I am fully persuaded by Dwight's reading of this verse and thank him for his comments at the manuscript stage of this book. In fact I want to thank Dwight for his comments on at least one other issue as well. They have improved my case no end.

My thanks must also go to the people of St Andrew's Church Chorleywood. When I gave a sermon version of this book on Easter Day 2005 a number of people urged me to turn it into a book-length study. I would never have thought of that had I not been encouraged by some wonderfully receptive listeners that memorable evening. My gratitude for my congregation is immense.

Dr Mark Stibbe, October 2007

# Foreword

Though last in New Testament sequence, the fourth gospel surely holds first place in the hearts and minds of most Christians. Of all the gospels, John's is the most read, cherished and oft-cited. If a single book of the Bible is to be distributed in pamphlet or tract form, invariably it will be the gospel of John. If any verse of the Bible is more memorised than John 3:16 – 'For God so loved the world . . .' – it is hard to imagine what it would be.

The fourth gospel is a literary masterpiece and a theological *tour de force*. Its profound and unambiguous identification of Jesus of Nazareth with the eternal Word of God incarnate in space and time has informed Christian theology from the earliest centuries.

At a more down-to-earth level, John's storytelling has inspired readers in every generation. His stories have brisk pace matched with a clarity that is always compelling. We don't easily forget, for example, Jesus' encounter at night with a devout spiritual leader in Israel named Nicodemus; or his mysterious action of writing in the dust when confronted by men intent on punishing a woman caught in adultery; or, the subject of the present volume, the risen Lord's encounter with a distraught Mary Magdalene in a garden, next to an empty tomb, and his puzzling retort to her, 'Don't touch me.'

The fourth gospel holds keen interest for scholars as well. Indeed a veritable revolution in Johannine studies has occurred in recent decades – a sweeping reassessment supported in no small measure by the historic discovery of the Dead Sea Scrolls and the fertile Jewish and Christian scholarship that sprang from there.

Classic Christian scholarship has viewed John's gospel as being a late work (second to third centuries) that reflects a thoroughly Hellenised (Greek philosophical) worldview. In marked contrast, the fourth gospel today is widely held to be a first-century composition that is indelibly Hebraic in character and composition.

John's theology, archaeology and spirituality are quite at home within the diverse but vibrant mix of Second Temple Judaisms. One need not look to the west and the 'sons of Greece' for interpretative keys to the fourth gospel; they are better to be found in the hands of the 'sons of Zion' and Jewish hermeneutics.

One distinguished scholar, noted for his work on the Dead Sea Scrolls, goes so far as to claim that the gospel of John is the 'most Jewish of all the gospels'. That conclusion probably overstates the evidence, but what is abundantly clear now is that the fourth gospel is in fact a Jewish document written to a Jewish audience using Hebraic categories of thought and subtle Hebraic literary techniques.

This contemporary scholarship forms the backdrop to the present volume by the Revd Dr Mark Stibbe.

Stibbe is an accomplished student of the fourth gospel. (It was in fact the subject of his doctoral dissertation.) But what he has written here is anything but a dry academic tome. *The Resurrection Code* reads like a well crafted mystery that carries the reader along with successive intrigues, hints and clues to a truly satisfying resolution that leaves the faithful both informed and inspired.

With the adroitness of a skilled sleuth, Stibbe sorts out various puzzles in the 'Easter enigma' recorded in chapter 20 of the fourth gospel. In one of the most charming literary compositions in the Bible, indeed of all literature, John recounts the astonishing story of the fervent Mary Magdalene discovering an empty tomb where Jesus had lain, illuminated by two radiant angels, and then, in a poignant moment often dramatised in Renaissance art, encountering her risen and transformed Lord in the garden. As the first witness of his resurrection, Mary is sent by the Lord to tell the apostles the good news, which she does in the memorable words, 'I have seen the Lord!'

The genius of *The Resurrection Code* is the way Stibbe enables the reader to see this familiar story through the Hebraic lenses of a devout first-century Jew steeped in the Hebrew Scriptures. The sacred tongue of Israel is inherently evocative, and the Jewish mind delights in biblical images and allusions that evoke imaginative associations and spiritual revelations. All this is part of John's world and is reflected in his gospel.

Stibbe in effect 'decodes' the Hebraic matrix behind the fourth gospel for the reader. He sensitises us to the 'inter-textual echoes with the Old Testament' and in the process, among other things, discloses fascinating and even startling discoveries about Jesus' resurrection and his encounter with his devout disciple, Mary Magdalene.

In *The Resurrection Code* we learn, for example,

- who is the author of the fourth gospel
- the identity and possible background of the mysterious figure (mentioned nowhere else in the New Testament) that John repeatedly refers to as 'the disciple whom Jesus loved'

- the likely timing of Jesus' resurrection from the grave and encounter with Mary (as against the conventional Sunday sunrise scenario)
- why John's gospel (unlike the other gospels) points out details of Jesus' grave clothes left behind in the tomb and what they signify
- how two angels posted at each end of the slab where Jesus lay may supply an interpretative key that unlocks the deeper meaning of Jesus' enigmatic encounter with Mary Magdalene
- why Jesus says to Mary, 'Do not touch me!' when later he invites the apostle Thomas to touch his hands and side

Reading *The Resurrection Code* is a stimulating experience. The adventure of finding 'secrets' that John has embedded in his gospel will appeal to everyone with an inquisitive mind. And the fresh insights into the significance of the resurrection of Jesus of Nazareth will edify people of faith.

One last comment: I especially appreciate Stibbe's respectful and enlightening treatment of the other key figure in John 20: Mary Magdalene. It is about time someone gave this remarkable woman her due. For far too long she has been ignored, misrepresented and maligned.

Within church history this devoted disciple from Magdala has been under-appreciated and ignored (eclipsed perhaps by all the attention given to the Virgin Mary), while in spurious Gnostic gospels and fallacious 'historical novels' such as *The Da Vinci Code,* as well as in movies and rock operas, she has been overly sensationalised.

*Miryam HaMagdalit* is one of the most intriguing women in the Bible. She was one of the Galilean disciples of *Yeshua* (Jesus) who followed him from the beginning, and along with other women disciples she supported his itinerant ministry out of her own means. She walked with the Lord to Jerusalem, was present at his crucifixion and was the first disciple – even ahead of the apostles – to encounter the risen Lord and speak with him. Sent by the Lord to the 'sent ones' (apostles) to announce his resurrection, Mary became in effect *apostola apostolorum* (apostle to the apostles). Her significance should not be overlooked.

Stibbe wisely assesses Mary's character, influence and importance not only to the apostles but to the whole church. He corrects some longstanding and widespread misconceptions about her in Christian history, and rightfully counters the misrepresentations of her by sectarian groups and the artistic guild. He restores Mary the Magdalene to a proper place of prominence and rightful respect.

*The Resurrection Code* is a masterful tale of love, triumph, intrigue and profound mystery. Stibbe's 'decoding' of the twentieth chapter of the fourth gospel gives me a renewed appreciation of this most wonderful of stories. I cannot say that I fully concur with every conclusion Stibbe draws, but I can say that I thoroughly enjoyed reading this book – and that I am better biblically informed and spiritually edified for having done so. An adventure awaits you!

Dr Dwight A. Pryor
Centre for Judaic-Christian Studies
Dayton, Ohio, and Jerusalem

# Introduction

When I was a boy I decided that my hero was Sherlock Holmes. His skill at deciphering the most complex codes deeply impressed me. His ability to infer a person's history and character from the tiniest clues was compelling. His relentless pursuit of his quarry ('The game's afoot!') was always exciting. Everything about his mind fascinated me. I wanted to be like Holmes when I grew up. I wanted to be a detective, or a criminal lawyer, and uncover the secrets that others carefully conceal.

Eventually, I did grow up (at least physically), and instead of becoming a policeman or a barrister I became a vicar and a biblical scholar! On the face of it, these two worlds might appear to have absolutely nothing to do with each other. But in fact this is not true. I cut my teeth as a scholar doing a doctoral dissertation on John's gospel. As I delved deeper into the text of this timeless narrative I began to realise that there are many parallels between what Holmes did and what a scholar has to do with the fourth gospel. Not everything in John's narrative is as it seems. There are secrets hidden beneath the surface – secrets that have to be perceived not only with the tools of historical and literary criticism but also with the illumination of the one John's gospel calls 'the Spirit of truth' (Jn. 14:17). The more I studied it, the more

I came to see that John's gospel is a coded or encrypted
text; it requires a Spirit-inspired form of literary detective
work to unlock it!

One of the greatest commentators on John in recent
decades has been the Catholic scholar Father Raymond
Brown. Brown wrote what I regard as the finest commentary on John to be published in the twentieth century, his
Anchor Bible commentary published in two volumes
(1966 and 1970 respectively). Brown's ability to appreciate
both the literary and the historical features of the text was
in my view unmatched. I well remember meeting Father
Brown when he and I were participating in the John
seminar group at an annual Society of Biblical Literature
gathering when it was held in the UK. It was an immense
privilege and I recall how impressive he was, both in
terms of intellectual acumen and personal humility.
When he died in 1998, the world lost one of the greatest
students of the fourth gospel, certainly from within the
Catholic world.

Father Brown saw the connection between studying
the fourth gospel and criminal detection – which, given
his name, is perhaps rather apt. In the introduction to
volume 1 of his commentary (which deals with John
chapters 1 – 12), Brown made a comment about this
which warmed my heart:

> It is notorious that many biblical scholars are also
> passionate readers of detective stories. These two
> interests come together in the quest to identify the
> author of the Fourth Gospel.[1]

Here a leading expert on John gave voice to exactly what
I was experiencing in my doctoral research and in my
post-doctoral writing and lecturing. Studying John is
like detective work, and not just in the context of its

authorship (the topic Father Brown singles out), but in just about every aspect.

What is it about John's gospel that makes it such a rich quarry for literary detection? It is the fact that the narrator, while exhibiting an almost omniscient perspective, at the same time withholds knowledge and information from the reader. On the one hand this narrator has access to a heavenly vantage point: his story begins 'in the beginning', in reality, 'before the beginning (of time)', when the Word was God and the Word was with God. This is a perspective that implies a very privileged degree of divine knowledge. On the other hand, while having access to such knowledge, the narrator chooses not to divulge everything in the telling of his story of Jesus. While no tale can be told in its entirety, the narrator leaves gaps at certain points. Indeed, the motto for any reader of the fourth gospel should really be what is constantly declared on London underground trains: 'Mind the gap!'

This brings me to this present work, *The Resurrection Code*, subtitled 'Mary Magdalene and the Easter Enigma'. The penultimate chapter of the fourth gospel provides an account of an episode involving Mary Magdalene – a female disciple who has attracted a great deal of attention in recent decades. While John 20:1–18 provides the most detailed insight into Mary Magdalene provided in any of the four New Testament gospels, it also raises intriguing questions for the reader. In other words, it conceals and reveals at the same time.

Here is the Bible's account of Mary Magdalene's meeting with her risen Lord:

> *Now on the first day of the week Mary Magdalene went to the tomb early, while it was still dark, and saw that the stone had been taken away from the tomb. Then she ran and came to Simon Peter, and to the other disciple, whom*

Jesus loved, and said to them, 'They have taken away the Lord out of the tomb, and we do not know where they have laid Him.'

Peter therefore went out, and the other disciple, and were going to the tomb. So they both ran together, and the other disciple outran Peter and came to the tomb first. And he, stooping down and looking in, saw the linen cloths lying there; yet he did not go in. Then Simon Peter came, following him, and went into the tomb; and he saw the linen cloths lying there, and the handkerchief that had been around His head, not lying with the linen cloths, but folded together in a place by itself. Then the other disciple, who came to the tomb first, went in also; and he saw and believed. For as yet they did not know the Scripture, that He must rise again from the dead. Then the disciples went away again to their own homes.

But Mary stood outside by the tomb weeping, and as she wept she stooped down and looked into the tomb. And she saw two angels in white sitting, one at the head and the other at the feet, where the body of Jesus had lain. Then they said to her, 'Woman, why are you weeping?'

She said to them, 'Because they have taken away my Lord, and I do not know where they have laid Him.'

Now when she had said this, she turned around and saw Jesus standing there, and did not know that it was Jesus. Jesus said to her, 'Woman, why are you weeping? Whom are you seeking?'

She, supposing Him to be the gardener, said to Him, 'Sir, if You have carried Him away, tell me where You have laid Him, and I will take Him away.'

Jesus said to her, 'Mary!'

She turned and said to Him, 'Rabboni!' (which is to say, Teacher).

Jesus said to her, 'Do not cling to Me, for I have not yet ascended to My Father; but go to My brethren and say to

> them, "I am ascending to My Father and your Father, and
> to My God and your God."'
>   Mary Magdalene came and told the disciples that she
> had seen the Lord, and that He had spoken these things to
> her. (Jn. 20:1–18)

On the face of it, everything seems to be fairly clear in this story. It is a simple and poignant recognition scene in which Mary Magdalene, in a state of deep grief, comes to recognise that the man she is speaking to is not a gardener but rather the rabbi whose death she is mourning. At the same time, any reader familiar with the other three New Testament gospels, not to mention the rest of John's gospel, will not be content with a quick, emotive reading like this. For the more informed reader, this account raises a number of interesting questions.

For example, why is it that the narrator is so precise about the number and nature of the grave clothes in verses 6 and 7? None of the other New Testament gospels mentions the grave clothes (apart from Luke's gospel). Why, in a gospel not noted for the description of precise narrative details, does John's gospel include these items?

Here is another example. Why is the narrator so keen to mention not only that there are two angels but also that they are positioned at each end of the stone slab where Jesus' body had been lying? Why are the angels posing like this? What is it that the narrator is trying to convey through this choreography? The gospels of Mark, Matthew and Luke do not mention this detail. Why does John?

And finally, why is it that the risen Jesus tells Mary Magdalene that she cannot touch, or more accurately 'hold on to', him? What is it about Jesus at this point that means that physical contact is not permissible? Jesus gives his own answer when he says, 'I am ascending to my Father'. But what kind of answer is this when we know from the Book of Acts (chapter 1) that Jesus did not ascend to heaven on the first Easter morning but rather forty days later?

In this book about Jesus' appearance to Mary Magdalene I want to pursue these questions and follow up the 'leads' and 'clues' left by the text. It is my view that what we have in John 20:1–18 is a narrative full of codes that require careful and robust analysis if they are to be decrypted. For those who are fascinated by Mary Magdalene, there is a treasure trove of revelation about her in store for us. For those who are intrigued by Jesus, there are insights about this rabbi that will take us way beyond what the surface of the text would suggest. Indeed, our reading will take us right into the most holy place of the throne room in heaven.

So, put on your deerstalker, take up your 'churchwarden' pipe and find your magnifying glass.

'The game's afoot!'

*I will give you the treasures of darkness*
*And hidden riches of secret places,*
*That you may know that I, the LORD,*
*Who call you by your name,*
*Am the God of Israel.*

Isaiah 45:3

# 1

# The Scarlet Woman

For centuries she has been depicted with long red hair, reaching out with passionate longing for Jesus outside the garden tomb from which he has just emerged. I am referring of course to Mary Magdalene, one of the most intriguing characters of the New Testament and one of the favourite subjects of painters, poets and storytellers over many centuries.

Take for example the painting by Alexander Andreyevich Ivanov which hangs in the Russian Museum in St Petersburg and is entitled 'The Appearance of Christ to Mary Magdalene' and dates from 1835 (http://www.abcgallery.com/I/ivanov/ivanov3.html). Ivanov was a painter who tried to revive the neo-classical style. His version of the encounter was highly regarded by his sponsors but Ivanov himself viewed it as a mere 'corn cob'.

There are a number of things to note about Ivanov's painting.

First of all Mary Magdalene's uncovered hair. While other Marys (such as Mary the mother of Jesus) appear in religious paintings with their hair covered, Mary Magdalene does not. This is telling, because any woman who had her hair loose and uncovered was regarded as a prostitute.

Long unkempt hair was also associated with deep repentance, as if the sorrow over sin had completely obscured the day-to-day responsibilities of grooming. Mary Magdalene has had the reputation of being a penitent prostitute for nearly two thousand years in the Western churches. Though the historical justification for this is very questionable, this did not stop a host of painters highlighting Mary's crowning glory – long, flowing, uncombed hair – as a symbol of her godly sorrow.

But it is not just the length of Mary Magdalene's hair but the colour of it which is remarkable. Sometimes she is painted as a brunette, even as a blonde, but most often, as here, as a redhead. Red is symbolic of passion. The red colours of her hair and dress suggest a history of sexual passion. Phrases still used today – such as a 'scarlet woman', or 'the red light district' – point to this colour association. Dan Brown picks up on this ancient connection by depicting his female protagonist in *The Da Vinci Code* – a woman related to Mary Magdalene – as a redhead.

This, then, is the classic portrayal of Mary Magdalene. But is it true to history? Who really was Mary Magdalene? And what was her relationship with Jesus? *The Resurrection Code* seeks to answer these questions by focusing on one particular source, the gospel according to John, and in particular the memorable scene on the first Easter Sunday morning, when Mary met her risen Lord.

## An Enigmatic Figure

In John's gospel she emerges out of nowhere. Having been invisible for the first eighteen chapters, suddenly she appears. She is simply referred to as Mary Magdalene – and she is mentioned as someone who requires no introduction. As John 19:25 reports,

*Now there stood by the cross of Jesus His mother, and His mother's sister, Mary the wife of Clopas, and Mary Magdalene.*

There are four women mentioned here. Only one of these has been referred to before, 'the mother of Jesus'. She is never called Mary in John, perhaps because of the number of other people called Mary. She appears as early as John chapter 2, when Jesus attends a wedding at Cana in Galilee and she tells her son that the wine has run out (truly bad news at a wedding feast). In response to her demand, Jesus performs a startling miracle in which about 180 gallons of water are transformed into vintage wine. Thereafter the mother of Jesus appears at the Cross but not again in John's gospel. An anonymous follower known as 'the disciple whom Jesus loved', or 'the beloved disciple', takes her to his own home after Jesus' death and she is not mentioned again (Jn. 19:27).

As for Mary Magdalene, this is an entirely different story. Not only does she make an appearance in John 19, but in the next chapter she will be a critical actor in the drama of Jesus' resurrection. She will come to the tomb very early on the first Easter Sunday morning and find it empty. She will run to the disciples to tell them, whereupon Peter and the beloved disciple will rush to the tomb to find Jesus' grave clothes lying there – but his body gone. They will leave and Mary Magdalene will remain. She will weep outside the tomb before seeing two angels. Jesus will then appear to her but she will mistake him initially for the gardener. Then, as he mentions her name, she will recognise her master's voice and be overjoyed, clinging to him in desperate relief. Jesus will tell her to let go of him and commission her to go and tell the disciples that he is alive and that he is ascending to the Father. Then, as quickly as she appears in the gospel, she will disappear. As John 20:18 reports,

> *Mary Magdalene came and told the disciples that she had seen the Lord, and that He had spoken these things to her.*

And with that she is gone – the enigmatic female follower of Jesus who appears without introduction in John 19 and disappears without fanfare in John 20.

## A Woman from Magdala

So who is this mysterious Mary Magdalene? Much has been written about her – very much, in fact, especially lately. No follower of Jesus in the gospels has in recent years received as much attention as Mary Magdalene. While Judas is proving to be a source of great interest too, it is Mary Magdalene who occupies the greatest appeal in the first decade of the twenty-first century. Her comeback is nothing short of remarkable.

But who is she? One way to answer this question is to narrow it down and ask, 'Who is Mary Magdalene in the fourth gospel?' This is important because there are so many faces to Mary Magdalene – there's the mystical face, the legendary face, the artistic face, the feminist face, the fictional face, the devotional face and, of course, the *Da Vinci Code* face. With so many different angles of interpretation the possibilities for confusion are endless. It is therefore important to be more focused and ask ourselves, 'What is the face of Mary Magdalene *in the fourth gospel*? What do we learn about her from a close reading of John 19 – 20? What do we see of her 'in front of the text', in its final form?'

If we go to the very first reference in John there are a number of things to notice. It is worth quoting this verse again because there is much more here than meets the eye – a characteristic of John's storytelling as a whole. The narrator tells us in John 19:25, 'Now there stood by the cross of Jesus His mother, and His mother's sister, Mary the wife of Clopas, and Mary Magdalene.'

The last name in the list is Mary Magdalene. Mary – or more properly *Miriam* – is a common enough name in first century Judaism. But what about 'Magdalene' – what does that mean?

Some argue that 'Magdalene' is a nickname and that it derives from a Hebrew word, *migdal*, meaning a fortress or watchtower. Those who hold to the nickname theory propose that Mary Magdalene must have been either very forthright or very tall, and that she was known as 'Miriam the stone tower'. Jesus gave Simon Peter the nickname *Cephas*, which could be translated 'Rocky'. Why shouldn't he have done something similar with Mary?

This is possible. However, the usual interpretation is that 'Magdalene' refers to Mary's place of origin. Jesus was called 'Jesus of Nazareth'. The reason for this is that the name Jesus – *Yeshua* – was extremely common and it was therefore important to add the place of origin as a means of avoiding confusion. The name Mary Magdalene shows the same tendency. Mary was a favourite name for Jewish girls (we have already seen that there are three Marys mentioned in John 19:25). To distinguish her from the rest she was called 'Miriam from Magdala'.

So where was Magdala and what kind of place was it? It is probable that the Magdala referred to in Mary's name was Magdala Nunayya, which means 'tower of the fishes'. Magdala Nunayya was a town on the edge of the

Sea of Galilee which supplied fish to a number of places, including Tiberias. It was located in the area of Capernaum, where Jesus gathered at least twenty of his followers, including some of his female disciples. The Jewish historian Josephus refers to this town of Magdala as 'Taricheae', which means 'a place of pickling houses' (probably referring to its fisheries and to the local industry of fish preservation). This town was destroyed by the Romans during the Jewish rebellion against Rome in the late 60s AD. Our information about it comes not only from the writings of Josephus but also from the Jewish Talmud.

So there are two theories about Mary Magdalene's name – there is the nickname theory and the 'place of origin' theory. It is even possible that both are right, and that Mary Magdalene refers not only to the fishy town in Galilee but also to the stone towers in which freshly caught fish were stored. Either way, the nickname is hardly an exotic one. Referring to Mary as 'Mary the fish tower' or 'Mary from the fishing town' is decidedly less romantic than some of the portrayals of Mary in medieval and Renaissance art!

### A Faithful Disciple

As soon as we understand that Magdala refers to a peasant town in Galilee it casts a totally different light on Mary Magdalene. Gone is the stylised portrait of an urbane and wealthy woman; in its place we have a portrait of a woman probably not from Jewish high society. Mary Magdalene was not a woman of standing in the modern sense but most likely came from the peasant class of Galilee. She was someone who had chosen to follow Jesus. In Luke's gospel we learn that she became a disciple because she had been tormented by evil spirits and Jesus had set her free through exorcism (a ministry for which he was well known). Luke 8:1–3 records

*Now it came to pass, afterward, that He went through every city and village, preaching and bringing the glad tidings of the kingdom of God. And the twelve were with Him, and certain women who had been healed of evil spirits and infirmities – Mary called Magdalene, out of whom had come seven demons, and Joanna the wife of Chuza, Herod's steward, and Susanna, and many others who provided for Him from their substance.*

Mary Magdalene was a woman who followed Jesus out of deep gratitude. She had experienced a great liberation when Jesus had ministered to her. Her response was to leave everything behind and follow Jesus. With a number of other women (also the recipients of Jesus' healing and exorcisms) Mary Magdalene travelled with Jesus. With these women and a number of other people, she provided for the itinerant band at the heart of this new Jesus movement and she did so, as the others did, 'from their substance'. This does not necessarily mean that she was rich, 'a woman of substance'. The word in the original Greek literally means 'out of the things owned' or 'the things to hand'. Mary Magdalene gave everything to her Rabbi Jesus, whom she loved and revered as the one who had emancipated her from spiritual and no doubt social chains. It may not have been much in material terms, but it was all she had.

So Mary Magdalene was a devoted female follower of Jesus. She may not have been a woman of standing in the social and material sense, but she was in the spiritual sense. Mary Magdalene stood with Jesus. This is reinforced in John 19:25 when the narrator tells us that 'there *stood* by the cross of Jesus His mother, and His mother's sister, Mary the wife of Clopas, and Mary Magdalene'. The word 'stood' is more than just an indicator of the posture of the four women mentioned here. It is an indicator of their allegiance and fidelity. The verb 'stand' in John's gospel is used metaphorically as well as literally. It is used of a number of characters to point to whether they are faithful followers of Jesus or not. It is used to pose a vital question to the reader: 'Where do YOU stand?'

The verb 'stand' (*histemi* in the Greek) is used twenty times in John's gospel as a whole. At the beginning of the story of Jesus' suffering and death, the narrator tells us in his account of the arrest of Jesus, 'Judas, who betrayed Him, also *stood* with them' (Jn. 18:5). Who did the narrator mean by 'them'? He meant the arresting party, comprising officials from the chief priest and Roman soldiers. Here the narrator emphasises that Judas stood with Jesus' enemies. He stood with them physically and he stood with them spiritually.

A little later on in John's passion narrative it's Simon Peter's turn. Jesus has now been arrested and is being subjected to an informal, illegal interrogation in the house of a former high priest called Annas. John 18:18 tells us what Simon Peter was doing outside: 'Now the servants and officers who had made a fire of coals *stood* there, for it was cold, and they warmed themselves. And Peter *stood* with them and warmed himself.' Here Peter not only stands with those who stand against Jesus. He stands next to a charcoal fire rather than with the Light of the World.

Now we come to Mary Magdalene. She – with the other three women – stands with the crucified Jesus. They stand at the Cross. What a stark contrast with Judas Iscariot and Simon Peter. What a contrast with all the other male disciples, bar the beloved disciple. Only the mysterious male follower known by this affectionate epithet, 'the disciple whom Jesus loved', is present at the Cross. In John 19:26–27 Jesus sees the beloved disciple and tells him, in a poignant scene, to treat Jesus' mother as his own mother. He is the only male disciple standing at the Cross. All the rest are noticeably absent. It is the women who stayed close to Jesus, not the men.

So Mary Magdalene was a woman who stood with Jesus. In John 20 the word 'stand' will once again appear near Mary Magdalene's name. We will see in John 20:11 that 'Mary *stood* outside by the tomb weeping'. We will see how 'she turned around and saw Jesus *standing* there' (Jn. 20:14). At the time of Jesus' crucifixion and at the time of Jesus' resurrection, Mary Magdalene is still standing and she is standing with Jesus.

Who are we standing with? What do we stand for?

## A Feminine Icon

Given these comments about male and female disciples it is little wonder that Mary Magdalene has become such an important figure for those who engage in feminist readings of John's gospel. There is without doubt a contrast between men and women in John 19. This is intentional as well.

As we have already seen, the narrator is very specific in the choice of words in John 19:25:

> *Now there stood by the cross of Jesus His mother, and His mother's sister, Mary the wife of Clopas, and Mary Magdalene.*

A detail worthy of note here is the number of women. There are *four*. Why should that be significant? The answer has to do with the scene immediately before John 19:25, in verses 23–24:

*Then the soldiers, when they had crucified Jesus, took His garments and made four parts, to each soldier a part, and also the tunic. Now the tunic was without seam, woven from the top in one piece. They said therefore among themselves, 'Let us not tear it, but cast lots for it, whose it shall be,' that the Scripture might be fulfilled which says:*

*'They divided My garments among them, and for My clothing they cast lots.'*

*Therefore the soldiers did these things.*

From these words we can tell there were four men on duty at the Cross. We know this because the narrator tells us very specifically that they proposed tearing Jesus' only remaining possession, a seamless undergarment, into four parts, 'to each soldier a part'. We also know this because it was common practice for a crucifixion to be attended by a *quaternion* of Roman soldiers – a group of four men, including a centurion.

John 19 therefore offers a contrast between the four men who were crucifying Jesus and the four women who were standing with him in his hour of need. This is obviously not a contrast between male and female disciples, but a contrast between men and women in relationship to Jesus. At the Cross, it is the women who are portrayed positively. The only man who shows allegiance to Jesus is the beloved disciple. Simon Peter and the rest of the male disciples are nowhere to be seen.

Mary Magdalene is accordingly a faithful female disciple in a chapter where men in general and male disciples in particular do not come across very well. But then this is actually true of the gospel as a whole. John's gospel is in fact entirely consistent in its positive portrayal of female disciples. A number of passages deal with faithful women: John 2:1–11 (the mother of Jesus), John 4:4–42 (the woman of Samaria), John 11:1–44 (Mary and Martha), John 12:1–8

(Mary and Martha), the four women at the Cross (Jn. 19:25), and Mary Magdalene (Jn. 20:1–18). In every case we find strong women who have an intimate relationship with Jesus and who play a significant and often unconventional part in Jesus' ministry. As Sandra Schneiders has written, 'Whoever the author of the Fourth Gospel was, it was someone who had a remarkably rich and nuanced understanding of feminine religious experience.'[2]

Sometimes this 'feminine religious experience' is described in contrast to 'male religious experience', and in these instances the women fare better than the men. When I was writing my narrative-critical commentary on John, I noticed this in a particularly visible way in John 3 – 4. In John 3, a Jewish man called Nicodemus comes to Jesus by night but fails to understand Jesus or make the choice to follow him. In John 4, a Samaritan woman meets Jesus at high noon, eventually comes to understand who Jesus is, and becomes a witness to Jesus in her own town. In my commentary I listed the contrasts between these two encounters as follows:

| Nicodemus | Samaritan woman |
|---|---|
| Takes place in Jerusalem | Takes place in Samaria |
| Context is the city | Context is the countryside |
| Happens at night | Happens at noon |
| Focuses on a man | Focuses on a woman |
| The man is a Jew | The woman is a Samaritan |
| The man is socially respectable | The woman has a history of immorality |
| Nicodemus descends into misunderstanding | The woman comes to faith |
| Nicodemus fails to see Jesus as the world's Saviour | The woman and her town come to confess Jesus as 'Saviour of the world' |

What this kind of analysis highlights is the very significant and positive role that women play in the fourth gospel. They are not lifeless cardboard cut-outs that play no part in the mission of Jesus. Rather, they act as faithful witnesses, often when the men are noticeably absent or silent. To take just one example, in John's gospel there is no reference to Simon Peter confessing Jesus as the Messiah, the Son of God (as he does in the Synoptic gospels at Caesarea Philippi). Instead, the great confession of who Jesus is comes from the lips of a female follower, Martha of Bethany. In the beautifully crafted scene of Lazarus' resurrection in John 11, Jesus asks Martha whether she believes that he is the resurrection and the life. Her reply is adamant in verse 27:

*'Yes, Lord, I believe that You are the Christ, the Son of God, who is to come into the world.'*

No one else in the entire course of John's gospel makes such an overt declaration of faith and understanding.

It is therefore no surprise that some of the female characters in John's gospel have become iconic for those who believe that women have a vital role and a significant, indeed equal place in the Christian community. In this regard, Mary Magdalene has become the most iconic of all the female characters in John's gospel. She appears three times at the hour of Jesus' death and resurrection. These three passages are:

- John 19:25: at the Cross, supporting Jesus
- John 20:1–3: at dawn, going to the garden tomb
- John 20:12–18: later that day, encountering Jesus

This may not seem a great deal in terms of narrative space, but it is nonetheless immensely significant. Mary

Magdalene has a pivotal role at the very climax of the gospel story. She is at the Cross when men are absent. She is the first person to arrive at the tomb (not Simon Peter or any of the other male disciples). She is the first person to see the risen Lord. And she is the one to whom the risen Jesus gives the commission to tell the apostles that he's alive – a commission that has given her the noble title, 'apostle to the apostles'. She is therefore a very important figure in John's story.

All this serves to reinforce the point that Mary Magdalene is a fitting candidate for pro-feminine readings of the fourth gospel. One of the pioneers of such readings has been Sandra Schneiders. She wrote this in an essay on women in the fourth gospel:

> The Mary Magdalene material in the Fourth Gospel is perhaps the most important indication we have of the Gospel perspective on the role of women in the Christian community. It shows quite clearly that, in at least one of the first Christian communities, a woman was regarded as the primary witness to the paschal mystery, the guarantee of the apostolic tradition.[3]

As Schneiders goes on to conclude, reflecting on the fourth gospel's presentation of women as a whole,

> If the material on women in the Fourth Gospel was released from the shackles of a male-dominated exegesis and placed at the service of the contemporary Church, there is little doubt that it would help to liberate both men and women from any remaining doubts that women are called by Jesus to full discipleship and ministry in the Christian community.[4]

## A Mistaken Identity

Mary Magdalene appears out of nowhere at the time of Jesus' death in John 19, and she disappears after fulfilling Jesus' commission in John 20. This hardly amounts to much, yet this female follower of Jesus has become the subject of a quantity of books totally out of proportion to the number of gospel references to her. Studies about her have been legion in recent years – studies with titles such as *The Magdalene Legacy, The Secret Teachings of Mary Magdalene, Mary Magdalene – Christianity's Hidden Goddess, Unveiling Mary Magdalene, Searching for Mary Magdalene,* and *Mary Magdalene, Bride in Exile.* She figures prominently in various recent movies, including *The Passion of the Christ* and most notably Abel Ferrara's *Mary* (2005). She is central to the novel *The Da Vinci Code* by Dan Brown and *Mary, called Magdalene* by Margaret George. She has featured in an episode of the cult TV series *The X Files,* as well as *Millennium,* and appears in the TV series *Rescue Me* in conversations with the lead character. She has even been referred to recently in video games, comic books and popular music. From the shadows, Mary Magdalene has emerged front stage in bright lights and to a great ovation. In 2005 she was named by *Newsweek* magazine as the 'It Girl' of our times.

And yet for all this attention, there is still great confusion surrounding Mary Magdalene. Many have wrongly identified her as the unnamed sinful woman who washes Jesus' feet with her tears. Luke 7:36–38 introduces the woman in question:

> *Then one of the Pharisees asked Him to eat with him. And He went to the Pharisee's house, and sat down to eat. And behold, a woman in the city who was a sinner, when she knew that Jesus sat at the table in the Pharisee's house,*

*brought an alabaster flask of fragrant oil, and stood at His feet behind Him weeping; and she began to wash His feet with her tears, and wiped them with the hair of her head; and she kissed His feet and anointed them with the fragrant oil.*

Luke chapter 7 ends with Jesus telling his host, Simon, that the woman has indeed sinned much, but that she has also repented at his feet with godly sorrow, anointing his feet with the fragrant oil from her alabaster jar. Therefore her sins are forgiven, because she has loved much. To the considerable indignation of the Pharisees in Simon's house, Jesus then forgives the woman and tells her that her faith has saved her and that she can go in peace. Though her name is not mentioned, Luke praises this woman's desperate faith in Jesus.

At this point Luke chapter 7 ends, and Luke 8 begins with the reference to the women who followed Jesus. The list begins with Mary Magdalene, and it is this that encouraged some of the early church fathers in the west to suggest that she was in fact the anonymous woman mentioned at the end of Luke 7. This identification was formally stated by Pope Gregory the Great – the Pope associated with Gregorian chant – in a sermon about Mary Magdalene in the year AD 591. He declared:

She whom Luke calls the sinful woman, whom John calls Mary, we believe to be the Mary from whom seven devils were ejected according to Mark.

Pope Gregory went on to suggest that the seven devils were not literal demons but rather the seven vices:

- Superbia (pride)
- Avaritia (greed)

- Luxuria (luxury)
- Invidia (envy)
- Gula (gluttony)
- Ira (anger)
- Acedia (sloth)

These were summarised by the seven-letter acrostic SALIGIA.

However, there is a great deal of doubt about pretty well all of this. First of all, the woman at the end of Luke 7 is unnamed, whereas Mary Magdalene is obviously given a name. There is no good reason for saying that the woman at the end of Luke 7 was really Mary Magdalene but was not named in order to protect her reputation. Luke has no hesitation in stating at the start of chapter 8 that Mary had had seven demons cast out by Jesus, a statement that hardly presents Mary's former life in a good light. Why should he be so bashful about the fact that she was 'a sinner' and yet so unembarrassed by the fact that she had been demonised? There really is no sound reason for Luke making Mary anonymous in one passage and then naming her in the very next.

Secondly, the idea that the seven demons are symbols of the seven vices or deadly sins really does seem to be reading too much into the text, even allegorising it. Jesus was well known as a charismatic holy man who set afflicted people free from unclean spirits. These spirits are described as very real and destructive spiritual entities in the gospels, not as specific sins or negative character traits.

Thirdly, even though some theologians in the Western churches believed that Mary Magdalene was the unnamed sinner at the end of Luke 7, this has not been the case in the Eastern churches. The church in the east separated from the Western, Roman Catholic Church in 1054. In the Orthodox tradition Mary was never seen as the anonymous sinner in Luke 7 and consequently she was never regarded as a prostitute. In the east Mary Magdalene has always been highly regarded as a holy myrrh-bearer and as someone equal to the apostles. She is not tarnished in the east by any speculation about a former promiscuous way of life, but rather venerated as a person of the same standing as the apostles.

Finally, the Roman Catholic Church in the west eventually recognised how spurious the connection was between the anonymous sinner of Luke 7 and Mary Magdalene in Luke 8, and a formal declaration was made to this effect in the 1960s. In 1969 the Roman Catholic missal and calendar were revised. Some saints' days were axed because of lack of evidence for the relevant saint's existence. St Christopher was one of those who lost out. In addition, other saints had their entries reconsidered. Mary Magdalene was still regarded as a 'saint' but her reputation for being the unnamed harlot of Luke 7 was dropped once and for all. Not all Catholics have abided by this decision. Mel Gibson depicts Mary Magdalene as the sinner of Luke 7 in his movie *The Passion of the Christ*. At the same time, in most Catholics' eyes, Mary Magdalene has been cleaned up and has received something of a makeover.

## A Leading Light

Sadly, the portrayal of Mary Magdalene as a woman who had once been promiscuous has historically distracted many people from recognising her prominence and significance in the early church. The truth is Mary Magdalene is regarded by all four New Testament gospels as a woman of great importance in the Jesus movement – and indeed in the earliest Christian churches. There are eight occasions on which Mary Magdalene is mentioned in connection with other women in the passion and resurrection stories recorded in the four canonical gospels. In all but one of these lists Mary Magdalene is mentioned first.

*Some women were watching from a distance. Among them were Mary Magdalene, Mary the mother of James the younger and of Joses, and Salome. (Mk. 15:40, NIV)*

*Mary Magdalene and Mary the mother of Joses saw where he was laid. (Mk. 15:47, NIV)*

*When the Sabbath was over, Mary Magdalene, Mary the mother of James, and Salome bought spices so that they might go to anoint Jesus' body. (Mk. 16:1, NIV)*

*Among them were Mary Magdalene, Mary the mother of James and Joses, and the mother of Zebedee's sons. (Mt. 27:56, NIV)*

*Mary Magdalene and the other Mary were sitting there opposite the tomb. (Mt. 27:61, NIV)*

*After the Sabbath, at dawn on the first day of the week, Mary Magdalene and the other Mary went to look at the tomb. (Mt. 28:1, NIV)*

*It was Mary Magdalene, Joanna, Mary the mother of James, and the others with them who told this to the apostles. (Lk. 24:10, NIV)*

*Near the cross of Jesus stood his mother, his mother's sister, Mary the wife of Clopas, and Mary Magdalene. (Jn. 19:25, NIV)*

The only occasion when Mary Magdalene is not mentioned first in a list of women disciples is in the last passage referred to, John 19:25. However, John chapter 20 more than makes up for this by focusing exclusively on Mary Magdalene at the empty tomb, rather than on the other women who we know from both the other gospels and from John 20:1–2 were present. So in John's gospel, as in the others, Mary Magdalene is the pre-eminent woman disciple. Even Jesus' mother is left unnamed in John's gospel, so as not to draw attention away from Miriam of Magdala.

One cannot therefore escape the conclusion that Mary Magdalene was a highly regarded female follower of Jesus. In fact, she was almost certainly the most famous of all the women disciples, both in Jesus' day and in the subsequent years of the early church. This in part explains why an unofficial gospel was written about Mary several hundred years later. This gospel is called 'the Gospel of Mary' and it contains some interesting insights into a marginal group of more mystical Christians from the second and third centuries AD. The focus of this fragmented text is Mary and, although it is not specified, it has been argued that this is Mary Magdalene. This Mary is presented as someone who has special knowledge about Jesus:

> Peter said to Mary, 'Sister, we know that the Saviour loved you more than all other women. Tell us the words of the Saviour that you remember, the things which you know that we don't because we haven't heard them.'
>
> Mary responded, 'I will teach you about what is hidden from you.'

While there are no compelling grounds for regarding these as the words of the historical Mary Magdalene, the fact that she is cast in the role of someone with special revelation cannot be dismissed as pure make-believe. On the one hand, 'the Gospel of Mary' as a whole is not a faithful record of words actually spoken by Mary Magdalene and others. As Philip Jenkins – an expert on the hidden or Gnostic gospels – writes,

> Dating is critical in determining authority. And that is why a text like the Gospel of Mary can tell us a great deal about the early third century, when it was written, but nothing at all about the historical Mary Magdalene, who had probably died two hundred years earlier.[5]

On the other hand, while the details are clearly fictional, the overall picture of Mary as someone characterised by intimacy and insight may well be based on reliable historical memory. Interestingly, in the Gnostic gospels there is no hint that Mary Magdalene had formerly been a prostitute. Instead, we learn that in the eyes of at least one group she was seen as a leader and a teacher. Even though her actual teaching comes not from Mary herself but from those who believed that *gnosis* or knowledge was the way to salvation, the fact that she is so highly regarded probably does reflect an ancient veneration for the first lady of the Jesus movement.

## Secret Gospels and Gospel Secrets

In the final analysis we do not have to resort to the fanciful reports of the Gnostic gospels to see what a richly intriguing figure Mary Magdalene is. The New Testament gospels contain enough to tell us that she was a crucial and complex figure in earliest Christianity. Indeed, while many contemporary writers follow hard after *secret gospels*, I want to show that we have yet to unearth the *gospel secrets* about her. John's story of the Magdalene has, in particular, yet to be properly appreciated. This present study is an attempt to unearth the treasures hidden there.

This book is also written in order to help the reader delve deeper into the life-changing events surrounding Jesus' death and resurrection. In the chapters that follow, as we track Mary Magdalene's journey from the Cross to the tomb and from the tomb to the upper room, we will see that John has composed his passion and resurrection narratives in a way that requires attention and insight from the reader. In other words, there are codes here that need deciphering, especially in relation to Mary Magdalene and her Rabbi Jesus. John's Easter story is written to conceal as well as reveal, and its elusive qualities call out for an informed reader response. This is because there is what I call an 'Easter enigma' at the heart of the Magdalene narrative at the end of John's gospel. These codes tell us a great deal about Mary Magdalene and her role not only in the fourth gospel but also in the earliest church. They also tell us a great deal about Jesus of Nazareth, not least about the extraordinary and awe-inspiring transformation that he underwent early on the first day of the week, as he rose from the tomb and encountered the mourning Magdalene in the garden. In what follows we will make a journey into the very heart of the Easter mystery, seeing it through John's eyes and focusing on Mary Magdalene's unique experiences.

*All night long on my bed*
*I looked for the one my heart loves;*
*I looked for him but did not find him.*
*I will get up now and go about the city,*
*through its streets and squares;*
*I will search for the one my heart loves.*
*So I looked for him but did not find him.*
*The watchmen found me*
*as they made their rounds in the city.*
*'Have you seen the one my heart loves?'*
*Scarcely had I passed them*
*when I found the one my heart loves.*
*I held him and would not let him go*

Song of Songs 3:1–4 (*NIV*)

## 2

# Weeping in the Cemetery

The garden encounter between Mary Magdalene and the risen Jesus has been the inspiration for artists and writers for hundreds of years. One such writer was Rudyard Kipling. He wrote a short story entitled 'The Gardener', published in 1926. It is a moving tale about the aftermath of the First World War, when many relatives went looking for the graves of loved ones in France.

Kipling's story describes a woman called Helen who adopts her nephew Michael when he is a baby. She brings him up in a loving way, giving him the best opportunities she can afford. Michael grows up and is about to enter Oxford University on a scholarship when war breaks out and he takes a commission as a young lieutenant in a brand new battalion. Just after Michael has written to Helen that there is no cause for alarm he is killed. Kipling puts it thus: 'A shell-splinter dropping out of a wet dawn killed him at once. The next shell uprooted and laid down over the body what had been the foundation of a barn wall, so neatly that none but an expert would have guessed that anything unpleasant had happened.'

Helen receives the inevitable telegram telling her that Michael is 'missing' and waits for further news. 'Missing' always means 'dead', she figures, yet she exhausts every avenue to receive confirmation. In the end no one can help her, so she resigns herself to the fact that he is gone: 'Michael had died and her world had stood still and she had been one with the full shock of that arrest.'

After the war she receives notification that Michael's body has been found and is buried in France. She travels there and finds twenty-one thousand are waiting for proper burial. She has no idea where her nephew is buried. But a gardener is at work behind some headstones and, seeing her, he asks, 'Who are you looking for?' Helen gives the name of her nephew and the narrator reports that 'the man lifted his eyes and looked at her with infinite compassion'. He tells her to follow him. The story concludes, 'When Helen left the Cemetery she turned for a last look. In the distance she saw the man bending over his young plants; and she went away, supposing him to be the gardener.'

Kipling's story is a poignant one. It is all the more poignant when one learns that Kipling's 18-year-old son John had been killed in the Battle of Loos in 1915 and that his body was never found in Kipling's lifetime. Kipling wrote 'The Gardener' while he was travelling through France in 1925, visiting war cemeteries. ('One never gets over the shock of this Dead Sea of arrested corps', he wrote.) He took the last line of his short story from John 20:15, where Mary Magdalene mistakes Jesus for the gardener. It is to this story – also involving the missing body of a loved one – that we now turn.

## A Missing Body

According to John 20, it was early on the first day of the week that Mary Magdalene made her way to the tomb where Jesus' body had been laid, in a cemetery outside the city. This would have been a well known site – a place where the rich and famous reserved caves for their own burial and for their family members' burials. The narrator reports what happened in John 20:1–2:

> *On the first day of the week Mary Magdalene went to the tomb early, while it was still dark, and saw that the stone had been taken away from the tomb. Then she ran and came to Simon Peter, and to the other disciple, whom Jesus loved, and said to them, 'They have taken away the Lord out of the tomb, and we do not know where they have laid Him.'*

We are told that it was 'early', a word that points to a time-frame before dawn (see Appendix 2). The narrator adds that 'it was still dark'. Darkness in John's gospel signifies more than just the absence of light. It is symbolic of an oppressive and destructive spiritual reality, of the work of Satan, the adversary of God. Ever since John 13:30, when Judas left Jesus to betray him and the narrator remarked 'it was night', there has been a sense of Satan working to steal, kill and destroy (Jn. 10:10). But now, on the first day of the week, the darkness is about to be dispelled and indeed cast out (Jn. 12:31). With the raising up of the Son of Man, light is about to pour into the world, life is about to radiate from the tomb.

Mary Magdalene's reasons for visiting the tomb are not specified in John. From the other canonical gospels (Mark, Matthew and Luke) we learn that her motive for making this journey was to anoint Jesus' body. The Torah (the first five books of the Hebrew Bible) stipulated that relatives should bathe, anoint and wrap the dead body of their loved one, even if the person had been crucified. This does not seem to be Mary's motive in John 20:1–2.

We learn at the end of John 19 that Nicodemus had already attended to these duties on the Friday. John 19:39–40 reads:

> *And Nicodemus, who at first came to Jesus by night, also came, bringing a mixture of myrrh and aloes, about a hundred pounds. Then they took the body of Jesus, and bound it in strips of linen with the spices, as the custom of the Jews is to bury.*

If Jesus' body had already been anointed, why did Mary go to the tomb on Sunday morning?

Mary Magdalene is not portrayed in John's gospel in the role of myrrhophore, or myrrh-bearer. Her reasons for visiting the tomb are not overtly described; they form a 'gap' in the narrative. But two factors give us a clue as to why she went. The first is the emphasis later in John 20 on Mary's weeping. John 20:11 reads, 'Mary stood outside by the tomb weeping, and as she wept she stooped down and looked into the tomb.' Twice in one verse the verb *klaio*, to weep or bewail, is used. In the subsequent verses the risen Jesus – whom Mary Magdalene will not recognise through her tear-drenched eyes – will ask her, 'Why are you weeping?' (*klaio* again, in verses 13 and 15). Clearly – according to John's gospel – Mary Magdalene came to the tomb to mourn over Jesus, not to anoint his body.

A second factor in support of this is the Jewish custom of mourning at the site of a loved one's burial. This custom is evident in John 11, when Lazarus dies. It is interesting to note that *klaio* is used eight times in John's gospel: four times it is used of Mary Magdalene at the tomb of Jesus, and three times of the sisters of Lazarus, as well as the other mourners, at Lazarus' tomb (Jn. 11:31 and 11:33 (twice)). This mourning often went on for three days, reaching its height on day three. The reason for this intensification was that the dead person's soul was believed to leave their body on the fourth day, so the third day represented the last opportunity to bid farewell.

In John's story, it seems that Mary Magdalene came to the cemetery to weep over Jesus. The business of cleansing, anointing and wrapping Jesus' body had been done on the Friday afternoon. It was now early on the first day of the week, and on this third day after Jesus' death Mary came to say her final goodbyes. As she approached the tomb, however, she saw that the stone had been rolled away. This stone was probably wheel-shaped and had been rolled into place on a track at the entrance of the tomb. This sort of entrance was typical of the more sophisticated tombs reserved for wealthier people, such as Joseph of Arimathea. Mary observed that this stone had been 'taken away', or 'removed'. Her immediate assumption is that Jesus' body has also been 'taken away' or 'removed'. Distraught, she runs to the other disciples to share the news.

## The Race to the Tomb

Mary arrives at the house where Simon Peter and an anonymous disciple (the 'beloved disciple') are staying and exclaims, 'They have taken away the Lord out of the tomb, and we do not know where they have laid Him' (Jn. 20:2). This short, breathless statement contains many 'gaps'. For example, who are the 'they' being referred to by Mary Magdalene here? And for that matter, who are the 'we'?

If we attend to the 'we' first, it seems from this tiny detail that Mary Magdalene did not go to the tomb alone. The synoptic gospels tell us that Mary Magdalene went with other women.

*Now when the Sabbath was past, Mary Magdalene, Mary the mother of James, and Salome bought spices, that they might come and anoint Him. (Mk. 16:1)*

From this verse (and Matthew 28:1, Luke 24:1) we learn that Mary Magdalene was accompanied by at least one other female disciple of Jesus. When in John 20:2 she says, '*We* do not know where they have laid him,' it seems she is referring to one or more of these female companions. The narrator does not mention them overtly because he wants the narrative focus to fall on Mary Magdalene, not on the other women.

Then there is the 'they' that Mary refers to here. 'They have taken away the Lord out of the tomb.' In the Greek this is perhaps not as emphatic as in the English translations. The original word could be translated in a more passive sense, 'The Lord has been taken away.' Nevertheless, the word 'they' in English is perfectly permissible and points to people other than the disciples who have removed Jesus' body. The perpetrators that Mary could be referring to are the hostile Jewish leaders responsible for Jesus' death, the Roman authorities who carried out the execution, or grave robbers. Mary's view is that Jesus' body has been stolen by one of these parties.

Mary Magdalene addresses both Simon Peter and the beloved disciple and they respond immediately and without any indication of disbelieving Mary's testimony. John 20:3–4 reads

*Peter therefore went out, and the other disciple, and were going to the tomb. So they both ran together, and the other disciple outran Peter and came to the tomb first.*

Having run from the tomb to the two disciples, Mary Magdalene now causes the two disciples to run to the empty tomb. Although it seems Simon Peter left first, the beloved disciple catches up with Peter and overtakes him, arriving first at the tomb. No reason is given why the beloved disciple runs faster, but in verse 5 the narrator reports what happened when he arrived:

*And he, stooping down and looking in, saw the linen cloths lying there; yet he did not go in.*

The verb 'stooping down' indicates that the entrance to the tomb was at ground level and that sufficient sunlight had now entered the chamber for objects to be seen in its recesses. This revealed that the body of Jesus had indeed gone but that his grave clothes were still present. These grave clothes are the body wrappings mentioned in John 19:40. The presence of these grave clothes indicates that Jesus' body has not been stolen (why remove the clothes before stealing the body?). The fact that the beloved disciple can easily see them indicates that they were probably lying on a shelf or slab in the cave. But no clue is given concerning why Jesus' body is now missing, or how that body became separated from the grave clothes.

The beloved disciple does not enter but waits for Simon Peter to arrive. As the narrator says in verses 6–7,

*Then Simon Peter came, following him, and went into the tomb; and he saw the linen cloths lying there, and the handkerchief that had been around His head, not lying with the linen cloths, but folded together in a place by itself.*

Peter enters the tomb first. He notices something else besides the grave clothes – a detail unique to John's account of the empty tomb story. Peter sees what the New King James Version (NKJV) calls a 'handkerchief' that had been around Jesus' head. Other translations render this word 'head cloth'. It refers to a shroud wrapped around a deceased person's head. This word – *soudarion* in the Greek – is used only twice in John's gospel, here in John 20:7 in relation to Jesus, and in the story of Lazarus in John 11:44. In the case of John 11:44, the narrator tells us

> *He who had died came out bound hand and foot with grave clothes, and his face was wrapped with a cloth. Jesus said to them, 'Loose him, and let him go.'*

All this acts as significant background to John 20:7.

The dead Lazarus had been bound in both body cloths and a head cloth. As a result of Jesus' command, Lazarus is raised from death and emerges from his tomb. Jesus tells the shocked bystanders to 'loose' or untie Lazarus and release him from the restrictions of his burial clothes. Fast forwarding to John 20:1–10, no such thing occurs in Jesus' own case. Instead of being unwound from his body by a third party, Jesus' burial clothes seem to have been exited *from the inside out*, without being untied. The main body wrappings now lie flat and all together on a shelf in the sepulchre. The head cloth lies in a separate place from the body cloths, and neatly. This last phrase is not easy to translate. The NKJV renders the original verb 'folded together', but it could equally mean 'wound round in an oval shape' – i.e. in the shape it had had when around Jesus' head.

The beloved disciple now enters the tomb, suggesting that it was a cave-like structure which could be entered and exited without difficulty. The narrator tells us in verse 8

> *Then the other disciple, who came to the tomb first, went in also; and he saw and believed.*

The reader is not told what it is that the beloved disciple believes. Reading the narrative on its own terms might lead one to think that the beloved disciple now believed Mary Magdalene's report that Jesus' body had gone. But this would be a real anti-climax to the beloved disciple's quest! The more traditional interpretation is that the beloved disciple saw the body wrappings lying on the shelf and the folded head cloth in a different place and consequently believed that Jesus' body had not been stolen and that he had risen from the dead.

This belief did not, however, include full under-standing. The narrator states in the next verse, in an aside to the reader, that neither the beloved disciple nor Simon Peter understood from Old Testament prophecy that Jesus had to be raised from the dead. The narrator does not specify what these Scriptures were. This is not the main point. The point is that Scripture showed that Jesus *had to be* raised from death. Jesus' resurrection was a necessary and divinely planned event. The men did not understand this yet.

At this stage, while the beloved disciple believes that Jesus is resurrected, the same is not said of Simon Peter. While both disciples are said to see what was in the empty tomb, only the beloved disciple is said to believe.

With these remarks on seeing, believing and under-standing, the narrator brings an end to the first section of his resurrection narrative. He records, 'Then the disciples went away again to their own homes' (v.10). The phrase 'the disciples' refers to the two men, Simon Peter and the anonymous beloved disciple. The NKJV tells us that they went away again 'to their own homes'. That last phrase is not in the original Greek but is used by the translator to fill a gap. However, it is unlikely that either the beloved disciple or Peter returned to their own homes, because that would have meant a return to Galilee, at least in

Peter's case. A better translation would be, 'to the place where they were staying', referring to the city of Jerusalem, where we shall find them a little later in John 20:19–23.


## The Mournful Magdalene

With the departure of the two male disciples the narrative focus falls on Mary Magdalene once again. A second section of the resurrection narrative now begins. There is a curious thing here. Having featured in the first two verses of John 20, Mary is not mentioned in the next eight verses. Yet now in verse 11 we read

> *But Mary stood outside by the tomb weeping, and as she wept she stooped down and looked into the tomb.*

The previous verse reports that the men returned to the city. In the very next breath the narrator says, 'But Mary stood outside by the tomb.' No information is supplied concerning Mary's movements while the two men have been in the tomb. This is yet another example of a tantalising 'gap' left by the narrator. However, it seems from the word 'but' at the start of verse 11 that Mary Magdalene had also hurried to the tomb when the two disciples had run there (which is entirely to be expected) and that she was simply not mentioned because the spotlight in verses 3–10 was on Simon Peter and the beloved disciple. The way it is written (pluperfect, 'Mary had been standing') suggests that Mary was present all along. This is further indicated by the use of the word *pros* in the Greek, which denotes that Mary had been standing 'near to' the tomb.

As Mary Magdalene stands near the entrance to the

tomb, we begin one of the most moving and memorable scenes in the entire Bible. Mary stoops down and looks into the sepulchre. In verse 12 we are told what she sees:

*And she saw two angels in white sitting, one at the head and the other at the feet, where the body of Jesus had lain.*

Once again the emphasis is on 'seeing' but this time there is something different. While the two male disciples had seen the grave clothes and the head cloth, Mary Magdalene now sees two angels. Mary Magdalene does not recoil in fear or fall over in wonder. No reaction is recorded at all. She is said simply to observe these two heavenly beings, and notes in the process their exact position within the tomb – 'one at the head and the other at the feet, where the body of Jesus had lain'. In other words, she sees an angel at each end of the stone slab where the dead Jesus had been left on the Friday evening. No explanation is provided. Any reason why the angels assume this posture is left entirely to the reader to infer.

As Mary Magdalene observes them, the angels address her: 'Woman, why are you weeping?' In answer to this question, Mary Magdalene speaks for the first time in the gospel. She answers, 'Because they have taken away my Lord, and I do not know where they have laid Him.' Here she refers to Jesus as 'Lord'. This may be significant. Fifteen times in John's resurrection narrative (John 20 – 21) Jesus is referred to as 'Lord'. The understanding of the Lordship of Jesus arises precisely out of the fact that he has been raised from the dead. The resurrection of Jesus is the foundation of the claim concerning the Lordship of Jesus.

More than that, Mary Magdalene describes Jesus in personal terms, as 'my Lord'. In John 20 verse 2 Mary had said to Simon Peter and the beloved disciple, 'They have taken away *the* Lord out of the tomb, and we do not know where they have laid Him.' Now Mary repeats this statement but replaces '*the* Lord' with '*my* Lord' and says 'I' instead of 'we'. And as she utters these words the narrator moves from showing (letting Mary speak) to telling (addressing the reader directly).

> *Now when she had said this, she turned around and saw Jesus standing there, and did not know that it was Jesus.* (Jn. 20:14)

Having made her lament to the angels, Mary Magdalene turns. She not only turns around, she sees Jesus. However, one can see someone without seeing who they are. That is precisely the nuance here. Mary Magdalene looks at Jesus but does not recognise him. There may be several reasons for this. First of all, there is the fact that Mary is weeping and her eyes would have been filled with tears. Secondly, there is the fact that Jesus' resurrection body, while continuous with his human body, was now a spiritual body. As such it had an otherness about it that made it hard for even the most devoted of his followers to recognise it, at least to begin with.

Whatever the reason, the same sequence now begins all over again. In verses 13–14, the angels had asked a question and Mary had made her response before finally turning to see Jesus:

v.13a: question to Mary
v.13b: answer by Mary
v.14: Mary turns to see Jesus (but does not recognise him)

Now, in this second instance in verses 15–16, it is Jesus who initiates the sequence:

v.15a: question to Mary
v.15b: answer by Mary
v.16: Mary turns to see Jesus (and does recognise him)

In verse 15 Jesus asks the question the angels asked: 'Woman, why are you weeping?' Only he adds a new question: 'Whom are you seeking?' The word 'seek' is significant in John's gospel, used thirty-five times, often not just literally but as a metaphor for a person's deepest spiritual longings. Jesus' question connects with Mary Magdalene's spiritual quest for relationship with her Messiah. It is a question that harks right back to the beginning of the gospel, where Jesus asks two disciples, 'What do you seek?' (Jn. 1:38).

Mary does not recognise Jesus, supposing him to be the gardener. She therefore answers by repeating her statement, 'Sir, if You have carried Him away, tell me where You have laid Him, and I will take Him away.' This is now the third time that Mary has made this lament, only now she has changed the 'they' (as in 'they have taken his body away') to 'you'. Mary Magdalene is at this point unaware of the irony of her situation – that she is asking the very person whose body she is looking for.

As soon as Mary has spoken, Jesus says one word, 'Mary', and Mary turns (the same verb again). She now recognises Jesus by the sound of his voice and says, 'Rabboni', which means 'my rabbi', or 'my master'. It is a moment full of pure and ecstatic joy, a moment predicted by Jesus the night before he died in John 16:20:

> *Most assuredly, I say to you that you will weep and*
> *lament, but the world will rejoice; and you will be*
> *sorrowful, but your sorrow will be turned into joy.*

Mary hears just one word, and her sorrow turns to joy.

## Her Master's Voice

It is important here to pause and ask why it is that Mary
Magdalene recognises Jesus when he says her name as
opposed to when she sees him.

In John 10 Jesus had compared himself to a shepherd.
This was a surprising figure of speech because shepherds
were a despised profession, which is perhaps why Jesus
goes on to add that he is the *good* shepherd. In the first six
verses of John 10 Jesus explains the comparison in some
detail:

> *'Most assuredly, I say to you, he who does not enter the*
> *sheepfold by the door, but climbs up some other way, the*
> *same is a thief and a robber. But he who enters by the door*
> *is the shepherd of the sheep. To him the doorkeeper opens,*
> *and the sheep hear his voice; and he calls his own sheep by*
> *name and leads them out. And when he brings out his*
> *own sheep, he goes before them; and the sheep follow him,*
> *for they know his voice. Yet they will by no means follow*
> *a stranger, but will flee from him, for they do not know the*
> *voice of strangers.' Jesus used this illustration, but they*
> *did not understand the things which He spoke to them.*

This passage is vital for our understanding of John
20:1–18. Jesus says he is the shepherd who knows the
names of his sheep and calls them by name. This is the
point of Jesus simply saying 'Mary'. He is calling her by

name. At the same time, Jesus says that the sheep hear the shepherd's voice and they know his voice. This is what Mary Magdalene is doing at the garden tomb. She recognises the sound of her name on the lips of Jesus. Indeed, it is the sound rather than the sight of the risen Jesus that causes her to recognise who he really is. There may be an otherness about the appearance of his spiritual body, but his voice is still instantly recognisable, and Mary Magdalene identifies herself as a true follower by recognising the word of the one called the Word (Jn. 1:1). As Jesus says in John 10:27, 'My sheep hear My voice, and I know them, and they follow Me.'

And all this relates to how Jesus' followers will recognise and know him now that he has been raised from death and been restored to the Father in heaven. How do people know Jesus now that he cannot be seen physically? This is a question with which the whole of John 20 is preoccupied, especially in its focus on the relationship between seeing and believing. It is a theme that reaches its climax in the beatitude Jesus utters to Thomas in John 20:29, 'Blessed are those who have not seen and yet have believed.'

It is *hearing* Jesus that really matters now that Jesus can no longer be seen. The verb 'to hear' (*akouo*) is used fifty-three times in John's gospel. The noun 'voice' (*phone*) is used fifteen times. Recognising the voice of Jesus is therefore a critical reality for all those who would know Jesus and believe in him. As Jesus said to Pilate in John 18:37, 'Everyone who is of the truth hears My voice.' So hearing Jesus is essential for discipleship. Indeed, in John's gospel, hearing is more important than seeing. Hearing Jesus for oneself is a major factor in coming to faith ('We ourselves have heard Him,' Jn. 4:42). Going on hearing is a major factor in continuing faith (Jn. 10:4, 'The sheep follow him, for they know his voice').

The moment Mary Magdalene recognises the sound of her name is therefore vital. It points, in fact, to an epoch-making moment – the moment when the nature of the relationship between Jesus and his followers now changes. Up to this point the relationship was based on Jesus' physical and visible presence. Now it is based on his spiritual and invisible presence. But physical absence does not mean an absence of relationship. Far from it! With the coming of the Holy Spirit, whom Jesus talks about frequently in John chapters 14 – 16, the disciples will not be left as orphans (Jn. 14:18). Rather, they will have a different quality of relationship with the Father and the Son – a relationship of personal intimacy made possible by the indwelling of the Counsellor (Jn. 14:16–17, 23). Through the Spirit, disciples will know the living reality of Jesus' words in John 16:27 (NLT), 'The Father himself loves you dearly.'

At the word 'Mary', the relationship with Jesus therefore takes on a new form. It changes from a relationship based on seeing to one based on hearing, from a relationship based on bodily presence to one based on spiritual presence. As Mary recognises Jesus by his voice (not by his appearance), the transition between the pre-resurrection and the post-resurrection nature of discipleship is signalled.

## Apostle to the Apostles

And this is the message of the very next verse in John 20. It is a moment much loved by artists through the centuries and captured in paintings with the Latin inscription *Noli me tangere*, meaning, 'Do not touch me.' In John 20:17 we read

*Jesus said to her, 'Do not cling to Me, for I have not yet
ascended to My Father; but go to My brethren and say to
them, "I am ascending to My Father and your Father, and
to My God and your God."'*

This is a verse that has attracted more attention and
commentary than just about any other in the New
Testament. It prompts a number of questions. For
example, what is Mary Magdalene doing here? The NKJV
translates Jesus' command as 'Do not cling to Me.' This is
a much more accurate translation than 'Do not touch me.'
The second implies that Mary is not touching Jesus and
Jesus is warning her against trying. The first implies –
correctly – that Mary is already touching him, that in fact
she is holding on to him, and that Jesus is telling her to
stop.

Why is Mary holding on to Jesus? The novel *The Da
Vinci Code* has revived a view that Mary was in fact Jesus'
wife and that her actions in John 20:17 are to be seen in
terms of physical intimacy. However, there is no
compelling evidence in any of the New Testament
gospels for this. The evidence usually cited comes from at
least three centuries later, from the Gnostic gospels.
Reference is usually made to a statement in the Gospel of
Philip (a late third-century fiction) which speaks of Mary
Magdalene as Jesus' 'companion', a word which does not
translate as 'wife' (contrary to claims made in Dan
Brown's novel), and of Mary Magdalene frequently
kissing Jesus. These kisses did not necessarily involve a
mouth-to-mouth embrace as one of Brown's characters
dogmatically claims. The word 'mouth' is missing from
the manuscript in the Gospel of Philip. The kiss could
therefore be nothing more than the 'holy kiss' mentioned
in the New Testament as an affectionate greeting between
Christians. Claims that Mary's actions mean more are

symptomatic of our contemporary culture, which sexualises just about every relationship and every thing.

Mary is not embracing Jesus in the way a wife would a husband. She is holding on to Jesus because he had died and he has now reappeared. Mary Magdalene clings to the resurrected Jesus because she loves him not as a lover but as a devoted follower and friend. She simply does not want to lose him again. Furthermore, she has not yet realised that her relationship with him must now change – from seeing to hearing, from physical to spiritual presence.

Why then does Jesus tell her to let go? The answer is given in the very next statement, that Jesus is in the process of ascending to his Father – to the Father who can now be Mary's Father, and the disciples' Father, in a personal, intimate sense. Thanks to the lifting up of Jesus on the Cross, a way to the Father has now been opened up for all who love and obey the Son. Now the Father can be Father to all who know Jesus, not just to the Son alone. Jesus tells Mary Magdalene to stop clinging on to him because he is still in the process of ascending – in other words, he is still in that 'hour' of elevation that will make intimacy with the Father a reality for all who come to know the Son. She *must* therefore let go.

What this reading demonstrates is the importance of Jesus' words, 'I *am* ascending.' The present tense of this verb is crucial. The ascension of Jesus is not something that takes place forty days or so after this first Easter Sunday. That is the picture Luke gives in the Book of Acts. It is not one that John gives in his resurrection narrative and we must resist the temptation of reading John through Lukan spectacles here. Although, as we shall see, the two accounts can be harmonised, it appears in John 20:17 as though Mary Magdalene has encountered the risen Jesus at a sensitive moment, at a moment when he is in some way or other returning to the Father. What this suggests is a kind of intermediate state between Jesus rising from the tomb and Jesus appearing to his disciples, including Thomas, and even allowing Thomas to touch him. Something is still going on between Jesus and the Father that causes him to tell Mary Magdalene that she cannot hold on to him. Quite what that is, the narrator does not say. It is an example of another gap in the narrative.

With the process of ascension still occurring, Jesus tells Mary not only to let go but also to go to the brothers with a message. The message is that he is ascending 'to my Father and your Father, and to my God and your God'. When Jesus refers to 'the brothers', he includes sisters too. The important thing is that the lifting up of the Son of Man (which now incorporates this moment of ascending to the Father) has created a brand new family of faith in which disciples can now know God personally as their Father and one another as brother and sister. This is the message that Mary is given and it is this commission that has caused her to be known as the 'apostle to the apostles'. The narrator ends by saying in verse 18

*Mary Magdalene came and told the disciples that she had seen the Lord, and that He had spoken these things to her.*

This is the last we see of Mary Magdalene in John's gospel. She obeys her Lord. She announces the message to the disciples. The word 'announce' (translated 'told' by NKJV) is *angelein*, a verb which reminds us of the two *angeloi* (angelic messengers) at the start of the Magdalene narrative (20:11). She announces that she has seen the Lord and she relates what she has heard Jesus say. With that, a beautifully constructed scene comes to a close.

## A Tale Artfully Told

What are we to make of this story?

John 20:1–18 is gospel storytelling at its finest. Philip Jenkins puts it this way:

> For me, the post-resurrection encounters between Jesus and Mary Magdalene are not just superb as literature, they are among the most moving passages in religious scripture of any kind. Literally, my hair stands on end when I read them.[6]

The artistry of John's storytelling is very visible when we look at the structure, genre and characterisation in John 20:1–18. The structure is very simple – a panel with three sections, with the Mary Magdalene episodes framing the whole presentation:

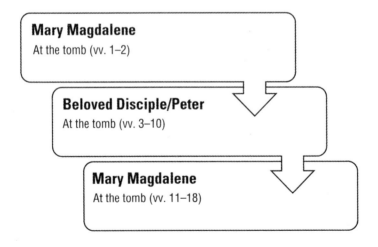

**Mary Magdalene**
At the tomb (vv. 1–2)

**Beloved Disciple/Peter**
At the tomb (vv. 3–10)

**Mary Magdalene**
At the tomb (vv. 11–18)

While Mary Magdalene is in the foreground in sections one and three, the two male disciples are in the foreground in section two. It is important for John to have the two men present. In Deuteronomy 19:15 we are told that 'by the mouth of two or three witnesses the matter shall be established'. Since John has already made reference to this principle twice, we may infer that he is indicating that there is the required number of reliable witnesses here (see John 5:31; 8:17–18).

If the structure of the passage is artful, so is the genre. On the face of it, John has described this incident using plot elements associated with the genre of Romance literature. Some of the features of this genre include the following:

- A lover seeks the body of their beloved at a tomb
- The lover finds that the tomb is empty
- The lover believes that thieves have stolen the body
- The lover later meets their beloved, who is alive
- The lover fails to recognise their beloved
- The sound of their voice triggers the recognition
- Falling to the ground, the two embrace[7]

One of the most famous examples commonly cited is the romantic novel of Chaereas and Callirhoe, told by Chariton in a book of eight sections. The story – dating from just after the time of Christ – is set in 400 BC in the city of Syracuse. Chaereas falls madly in love with the unusually beautiful Callirhoe, but when he wrongly suspects her of adultery he kicks her so hard she falls as if dead. She is placed in a tomb after her funeral. It then turns out that she is not dead after all, but in a coma. She wakes up just in time to find pirates robbing the tomb. They abduct her and take her to Miletus, where she is sold as a slave to Dionysius, who falls in love with her and marries her. She is too frightened to tell him that she is married to Chaereas and is bearing his child. Meanwhile, Chaereas learns that his beloved is alive and goes looking for her. He too is captured and turned into a slave by the Persians. When war eventually breaks out, Chaereas successfully leads a group of Egyptian rebels against the Persians, after which the lovers are reunited. They return to Syracuse giving thanks to Aphrodite, the goddess of love.

While there are some very broad similarities between this kind of novelistic fiction and John's storytelling, the differences are just as telling. For one thing, this story comes from the second century AD – at least one hundred years after John's. For another, Jesus really does die in John 19. It is not that he appears to be dead and is in a coma. Furthermore, the ending of the stories is markedly different. Chaereas and Callirhoe fall to the ground and embrace. As Chariton puts it, 'As they rushed into each other's arms they fainted and fell to the floor' (VIII, 1:7ff). In John's account, Jesus tells Mary Magdalene to stop holding on to her. The relationship that he has with her from now on must be a spiritual one, because he is returning to his Father. So, there are similarities with the genre of romance (including echoes of Song of Songs 3:1–5), but there are important differences too. These differences highlight John's commitment not only to romance but to reality – to what really happened.

If the structure and genre of this story are worth noting, so is the characterisation. If we focus on Mary Magdalene, the first thing we see is the amount of speech given to her. John's gospel gives far more space to the speech of female characters than the other three gospels. Mark's gospel records women speaking just five times, Matthew nine times and Luke eleven times. But in the fourth gospel we find twice as many references to women speaking as in Luke – twenty-two in total, involving Jesus' mother, the Samaritan woman, Mary and Martha of Bethany, the servant girl of Annas the high priest, and of course Mary Magdalene. John gives a voice to an impressive number of female characters:

| Reference | Character | Subject |
|-----------|-----------|---------|
| 2:3 | Mother of Jesus | 'They have no wine' |
| 2:5 | Mother of Jesus | 'Do whatever he says' |
| 4:9 | Samaritan woman | Water |
| 4:11–12 | Samaritan woman | Water |
| 4:15 | Samaritan woman | Water |
| 4:17 | Samaritan woman | Marriage |
| 4:19–20 | Samaritan woman | Prophecy/worship |
| 4:25 | Samaritan woman | The Messiah |
| 4:29 | Samaritan woman | The Messiah |
| 4:39 | Samaritan woman | 'He told me everything I did' |
| 11:3 | Mary and Martha | Lazarus' sickness |
| 11:21–22 | Martha | 'If only you had been here' |
| 11:24 | Martha | Death and resurrection |
| 11:27 | Martha | Confession of who Jesus is |
| 11:28 | Martha | Calling her sister, Mary |
| 11:32 | Mary of Bethany | 'If only you had been here' |
| 11:39 | Martha | 'He's been dead four days' |
| 18:17 | Annas' servant girl | 'You're a disciple of his' |
| 20:2 | Mary Magdalene | 'The body's gone' |
| 20:13 | Mary Magdalene | 'The body's gone' |
| 20:15 | Mary Magdalene | 'The body's gone' |
| 20:16 | Mary Magdalene | 'Rabboni' |

While all four gospels record Mary Magdalene's pivotal

role in the resurrection of Jesus, only John's gospel reports her speaking, and on four occasions:

> *'They have taken away the Lord out of the tomb, and we do not know where they have laid Him.' (Jn. 20:2)*
>
> *She said to them, 'Because they have taken away my Lord, and I do not know where they have laid Him.' (Jn. 20:13)*
>
> *She, supposing Him to be the gardener, said to Him, 'Sir, if You have carried Him away, tell me where You have laid Him, and I will take Him away.' (Jn. 20:15)*
>
> *Jesus said to her, 'Mary!' She turned and said to Him, 'Rabboni!' (which is to say, Teacher). (Jn. 20:16)*

What is immediately clear from these references is Mary Magdalene's preoccupation with the location of the body of Jesus. Three out of the four references to her speaking are taken up with this theme. The third occasion sets up the irony of Mary asking Jesus about the location of his own body. This in itself has caused some debate. Is Mary Magdalene being portrayed negatively here, as a victim of the common theme of 'misunderstanding' in John's gospel? J.D. Crossan is particularly dismissive, saying, 'Mary gets to give the wrong interpretation of the empty tomb three times: to the disciples, to the angels, and finally to Jesus himself. She does not even recognise Jesus when he appears to her, at least until he addresses her.'[8]

But this is really unwarranted. Mary Magdalene recognises Jesus immediately he mentions her name, and this is the point as far as John is concerned. Mary is being presented here as being like the sheep that recognise their Shepherd's voice as he calls them by name (Jn. 10:3). There is no hint that she is portrayed as slow to understand once Jesus has spoken to her. The fact is, she is the very first person to meet the risen Jesus and she recognises him on the basis of hearing, not seeing. This is how friendship with Jesus must be for all post-Easter disciples. Mary Magdalene is a representative of this kind of faith.

This positive portrayal is further confirmed by the fact that Jesus gives Mary Magdalene the task of going to the disciples and giving them his message: 'I am ascending to My Father and your Father, and to My God and your God' (Jn. 20:17). As many have realised, the fact that Jesus is sending Mary Magdalene to the male disciples makes her an apostle to the apostles. So the fact that she is sent is significant enough. But then so is the content of what she is told to say. She is effectively told to proclaim the news that Jesus is returning to the Father. This means that not only is she the apostle of the Resurrection, she is also the apostle of the Ascension! And she is obedient to this charge. Verse 18 (which closes our story) reports that she went and told the disciples that she had seen the Lord and that he had spoken these things to her. Now, in addition to all the direct speech we have heard from her, a verse full of indirect speech is given. As Karen Thiessen says in her essay 'Jesus and Women in the Gospel of John', 'The Fourth Gospel portrays Mary Magdalene as having a claim to apostleship not unlike Peter's and Paul's. She, like them, saw the risen Lord and received from him the commission to go and preach the news of his resurrection.' She concludes, 'Rather than viewing women in terms of their roles of wife, mother and housekeeper as was common within Jewish culture, the Johannine Jesus views them as individuals capable of making important decisions and commitments.'[9]

John 20:1–18 is a tale artfully told. This is no careless and clumsy collage of memories from John's oral and written traditions. Rather, it is an episode beautifully reconstructed so as to highlight the significant role played by Mary Magdalene in the discovery of the empty tomb and the relaying of momentous news to the disciples. Mary Magdalene is the first person to encounter the risen Jesus and the first person to speak with Jesus after he has risen from the dead. The suggestion of John's dramatic and poignant presentation is that Mary Magdalene interrupted the risen Jesus at a critical moment in the early hours of the first Sunday morning, shortly after he had risen from the dead and just before he had gone to the Father. This moment was so critical that Jesus had to tell Mary Magdalene very firmly to stop touching or holding him, because he was ascending at that moment to the Father. This is a curious thing to say because eight days later (Jn. 20:26), the risen Jesus is still on the earth and is now telling Thomas to reach out and touch his wounds. What is Jesus doing on the first Easter Sunday morning that means Mary cannot touch him? This question cries out for an answer. As yet, a convincing explanation has not been given.

*It is the glory of God to conceal a matter,*
*But the glory of kings is to search out a matter.*

Proverbs 25:2

# 3

# A Tomb with a View

Sometimes a piece of writing can appear deceptively simple. Take this poem by Wordsworth as an example:

> She dwelt among the untrodden ways
> Beside the springs of Dove,
> A Maid whom there were none to praise
> And very few to love:
>
> A violet by a mossy stone
> Half hidden from the eye!
> Fair as a star, when only one
> Is shining in the sky.
>
> She lived unknown, and few could know
> When Lucy ceased to be;
> But she is in her grave, and, oh,
> The difference to me!

At first sight, this poem seems to be crystal clear. It is an elegy for a woman whom Wordsworth had either known personally or at the very least known about. When we reread the piece, however, some intriguing questions begin to surface.

In the first stanza, the poet tells us that Lucy (the subject of the piece) lived among ways that were untrodden. But how can a way still be a way if no one is walking on it? In the same stanza the poet says that there were none to praise Lucy. He adds that there were 'very few to love'. This is odd too. How can a person love someone without praising them? Either there were few loving and praising Lucy, or there was no one to love and praise her!

In the second stanza, more questions arise. How can a person be both like a half-concealed flower and at the same time like a shining star? The first image is indicative of hiddenness. The second connotes radiance. How can something be both obscure and obvious at the same time?

Then, in the final stanza, the poet begins by saying that Lucy lived unknown and that few could have known when she died. Here again there is a striking sense of a paradox. In the same line the poet uses the words 'lived unknown' and 'few could know'. Either someone is unknown or known. It cannot be both!

Summing up, Wordsworth presents a set of very incongruous contrasts: trodden/untrodden, obscure/obvious, and known/unknown. To these we might add the contrast 'alive/dead'!

So what is going on here? A poem that looked so simple turns out to be profoundly perplexing. Is this a genuine lament for a lost love? Or is it a game played with language? Does the word 'difference' in the last line indicate a sense of catastrophic loss? Or does it point to a game being played with the idea of 'differences'? Through a clever use of paradox Wordsworth leaves gaps in the text and it is these 'gaps' that create dynamism. The power in fact is in the gaps. As Wolfgang Iser explains,

Even in the simplest story there is bound to be some kind of blockage, if only for the fact that no tale can ever be told in its entirety. Indeed, it is only through inevitable omissions that a story will gain its dynamism. Thus whenever the flow is interrupted and we are led off in unexpected directions, the opportunity is given to us to bring into play our own faculty for establishing connections – for filling in the gaps left by the text itself.[10]

Wordsworth's 'Lucy' poem is a brilliant example of how an author can deliberately omit information in a text in order to engage the imaginative cooperation of the reader. Of course, there is a risk in this strategy. There is always the danger of the reader imposing meanings on a text that were never intended. At the same time, the intentional use of 'gaps' can woo the reader into a much deeper interaction which yields treasures not immediately visible. This is exactly what Wordsworth does in his poem about Lucy. And it is what John does in his simple narration of Mary Magdalene's grief at the tomb.

## A Gap Opened Up

John 20:1–18 is, in a sense, all about a gap. The narrative space that forms the focus of the reader's attention is the tomb of Jesus – a gap in a rock. The Greek word for 'tomb' is *mnemeion* and it is used nine times in John 20:1–11:

> *On the first day of the week Mary Magdalene went to the tomb early, while it was still dark, and saw that the stone had been taken away from the tomb. (Verse 1)*

*'They have taken away the Lord out of the tomb.' (Verse 2)*

*Peter therefore went out, and the other disciple, and were going to the tomb. (Verse 3)*

*So they both ran together, and the other disciple outran Peter and came to the tomb first. (Verse 4)*

*And he, stooping down and looking in, saw the linen cloths lying there; yet he did not go in. (Verse 5)*

*Then Simon Peter came, following him, and went into the tomb. (Verse 6)*

*Then the other disciple, who came to the tomb first, went in also. (Verse 8)*

*Mary stood outside by the tomb weeping, and as she wept she stooped down and looked into the tomb. (Verse 11)*

All the action in John 20:1–18 takes place at the tomb entrance. Mary Magdalene comes to the tomb. The beloved disciple and Peter run to the tomb. The beloved disciple looks but does not go into the tomb. Peter arrives and enters. The beloved disciple then goes in too. The two disciples leave and Mary Magdalene looks into the tomb. She sees the two angels and converses with them before she turns away from the entrance and faces Jesus. The story ends with her leaving the tomb to proclaim the news that she has seen the Lord.

The action of the entire piece revolves around a literal gap. The stone has been removed and now everything occurs at the lip of the tomb of Jesus. A gap is opened up – and the biggest gap of all is the empty space between the angels, where Jesus' body had been lying. Mary

Magdalene looks intently into this gap and penetrates the deepest of all mysteries. In a very real sense, this is a metaphor for the reader too. In reading we stand, Magdalene-like, before the gaps in an intriguing text.


## The Folded Grave Clothes

It is time now to identify some of the 'gaps' that are left by the narrator in the account of the empty tomb in John 20:1–18. There are a number of 'deliberate' omissions or 'gaps' here and it is these that create the sense of an 'Easter enigma'. The lack of explanation at a number of points is entirely deliberate. These gaps are used by the narrator to entice the reader into a far deeper reading experience than would otherwise be possible. This is a story that encourages rereading through the use of artful reticence.

The first example concerns the grave clothes discovered in the empty tomb. The full text reads as follows in John 20:4–8:

> *So they both ran together, and the other disciple outran Peter and came to the tomb first. And he, stooping down and looking in, saw the linen cloths lying there; yet he did not go in. Then Simon Peter came, following him, and went into the tomb; and he saw the linen cloths lying there, and the handkerchief that had been around His head, not lying with the linen cloths, but folded together in a place by itself. Then the other disciple, who came to the tomb first, went in also; and he saw and believed.*

Two things need to be noted about these grave clothes. The first has to do with the detail of their description. Two items are mentioned, the linen cloths (that would have covered the whole body) and the head cloth (the linen covering for the head). The first word, linen cloths, is *othonia* in the Greek, a word that is used four times in John but only five times in the New Testament as a whole (the other occurrence is in Luke 24:12). The word translated 'head cloth' is *soudarion*, which is used only four times in the New Testament: here in John 20:7, then again in the story of the raising of Lazarus in John 11:44, and twice in the writings of Luke (Luke 19:20 and Acts 19:12). These are specific words and point to a level of vivid description that is not always visible in the rest of John's gospel. Indeed, there are very few places where the narrator provides the kind of elaborate narrative detail that we find in John 20:4–9. Why do we find such precision here? Why does the narrator break from his usual strategy of drawing general rather than precise pictures?

The second thing to note is the uniqueness of this description. Compare John's account of the empty tomb with those found in Mark, Matthew and Luke. Mark's gospel never mentions grave clothes at the tomb. He does say that Joseph of Arimathea wrapped Jesus' dead body in a long shroud on Good Friday:

> *Joseph bought a long sheet of linen cloth, and taking Jesus' body down from the cross, he wrapped it in the cloth and laid it in a tomb that had been carved out of the rock. Then he rolled a stone in front of the entrance. (Mk. 15:46, New Living Translation (NLT))*

The word Mark uses here is *sindon*, meaning fine linen (a word he uses four times in Mark 14 – 15). But he says nothing of this fine linen shroud at the empty tomb.

In Matthew's gospel there is no mention of Jesus' grave clothes at the empty tomb on Easter Sunday morning, though Matthew follows Mark in describing Joseph wrapping Jesus' body in a linen cloth on Good Friday (Mt. 27:59).

In Luke the emphasis is on the women searching the interior of the tomb for Jesus' body. The striking thing for Luke is the way two angels materialise inside the tomb. Luke does mention linen cloths in the tomb (Lk. 24:12) but there is no mention of the position or the state of these cloths, and Luke does not make any reference to the *soudarion* or head cloth.

John alone is specific about the grave clothes in the tomb.

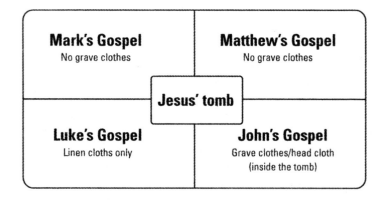

So why does John choose to focus on these two objects, the garment that had covered Jesus' body and the turban or head cloth? What is the significance of this very specific language?

A number of solutions have been proposed. One has to do with John's understanding of the resurrection body of Jesus. It has been argued that the narrator shows these garments lying flat on the stone slab, having collapsed neatly as the body of Jesus was no longer contained within them, and that the purpose is to show that Jesus' resurrected body can pass through clothes in a supernatural way. This new body can break out of garments from the inside out, leaving them neatly where the old body had been.

This is further confirmed when we look elsewhere in John's gospel. In John chapter 11, a friend of Jesus' called Lazarus dies. He is placed in a tomb and spends three days there. On the fourth day Jesus arrives and raises him from death. When Jesus shouts out the command for Lazarus to come out of the tomb, John describes the scene:

*And Lazarus came out, bound in graveclothes, his face wrapped in a headcloth. Jesus told them, 'Unwrap him and let him go!' (Jn. 11:44, NLT)*

What is striking here is the similarity between Lazarus' grave clothes and those of Jesus in John 20. Both have a whole-body garment and both have a head cloth. The difference is that Lazarus needs help getting out of his grave clothes, which are said to be binding him. Jesus, on the other hand, passes straight through his funeral garments unaided. This highlights the fact that what happened to Jesus was qualitatively different from what happened to Lazarus. Lazarus experienced temporary resuscitation. Jesus experienced permanent resurrection. Lazarus needed to be helped out of his grave clothes. Jesus simply passed through his.

Another solution has also been suggested. Some scholars argue that John has inserted this detail to prove that grave robbers could not have stolen Jesus' body. If thieves had come to the tomb they would have simply taken the body wrapped in the linen cloth and the napkin that had been around Jesus' head. They would never have bothered to unwrap Jesus so carefully before rushing off with their prize. They would certainly have been in far too much of a hurry to leave the head cloth neatly folded on the ground.

A third solution has been proposed to me by a friend interested in the Jewish roots of the Christian faith. She was told by an Orthodox rabbi in Jerusalem that the folded head cloth has to do with Jewish meal customs in the first century AD. The rabbi explained that if a guest at a Jewish table had enjoyed his meal, he would crumple the napkin and leave it in a heap on his place setting. That was a coded way of saying, 'I've really enjoyed the hospitality and I'd like to come back.' If he had not enjoyed the experience he folded the napkin and left it very neatly and deliberately on the place setting. That was a coded way of saying, 'I have not enjoyed this hospitality and I don't intend to return.' The rabbi proposed that Jesus left the folded head cloth as a signal that he had not enjoyed the experience and was not intending to return to the tomb, ever! Unlike Lazarus, Jesus was not going to return to the tomb to taste death again. His time in the tomb was a once for all experience.[11]

I like this third solution. It has the advantage of respecting the Jewish background of John's gospel writing. At the same time I have seen no documentary evidence as yet to prove that such meal conventions were in operation in the first century, or that John had such customs in mind in his description of the empty tomb. So far, no one has come up with passages from the Jewish literature of Jesus' day that clearly demonstrate this code.

While these solutions offer helpful insights, we are nonetheless left dissatisfied, with the feeling that there is more to these grave clothes than meets the eye, that the narrator sees something significant about them beyond their literal value. The reticence of the narrator leaves us with 'gaps', with deliberate omissions which entice us into asking questions. Is the narrator trying to tell us something significant in this description of the whole-body linen cloths and the turban or head cloth? Is there something symbolic about these garments in the religious imagination of the storyteller?

## The Two Angels in the Tomb

The second intriguing gap concerns the angels.

An angel is a messenger from God. The word angel comes from the Greek word *angelos* meaning 'a messenger'. According to the Bible, angels are intelligent heavenly beings whom God employs in his government of the world. While angels are ministering 'spirits', they always appear in human form when transmitting a divine message to men and women.

Angels attended the birth of Jesus. Some Christmas carols describe these appearances:

> While shepherds watched their flocks by night
> All seated on the ground
> The angel of the Lord came down
> And glory shone around.

> Words: Nahum Tate

While angels appear after Jesus has been born, they also appear after Jesus has died. Both at Jesus' birth as a baby and his emergence as a resurrected human being, angels make their appearance.

In Mark's account of the resurrection we find one angel at the tomb, who looks like a young man dressed in white. He is on the right-hand side of the tomb. Mark 16:5–6 says of the women

> *So they entered the tomb, and there on the right sat a young*
> *man clothed in a white robe. The women were startled, but*
> *the angel said, 'Do not be so surprised.' (NLT)*

In Matthew's gospel there is also one angel mentioned. This is an impressive celestial being described as 'an angel of the Lord'. Matthew reports in chapter 28 verses 1–4

> *Early on Sunday morning, as the new day was dawning,*
> *Mary Magdalene and the other Mary went out to see the*
> *tomb. Suddenly there was a great earthquake, because an*
> *angel of the Lord came down from heaven and rolled aside*
> *the stone and sat on it. His face shone like lightning, and*
> *his clothing was as white as snow. The guards shook with*
> *fear when they saw him, and they fell into a dead faint.*
> *(NLT)*

In Luke's gospel there are two angels. These are not in the tomb when the women enter the tomb but materialise as they look on. As we read in Luke 24:4

> *And it happened, as they were greatly perplexed about this,*
> *that behold, two men stood by them in shining garments.*

In chapter 20 of John's gospel there are two angels. Verse 12 is the key, where we read of Mary Magdalene

> *She saw two white-robed angels sitting at the head and*
> *foot of the place where the body of Jesus had been lying.*
> *(NLT)*

Summarising, we can begin to see the differences between the four accounts:

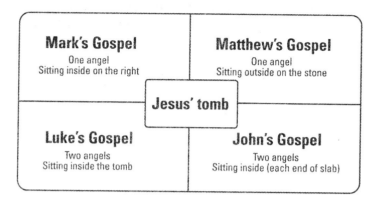

What is most interesting about John's account is the place of the two white-robed angels. They are said to be sitting at each end of the slab of stone where Jesus' dead body had been, 'one at the head, the other at the feet, where the body of Jesus had been'. But why do they assume this choreographed posture? Some have argued that the two angels situated either side of the dead Christ are the counterpart to the two criminals on either side of the dying Christ. But this is hard to prove. Much more compelling is the idea that the two angels are supposed to remind the reader of the cherubim – the supernatural angelic beings – either side of the Ark of the Covenant in the Tabernacle of Moses. In Exodus 25:17–20 we find the description of the Ark (my emphasis):

*You shall make a mercy seat of pure gold; two and a half cubits shall be its length and a cubit and a half its width. And you shall make two cherubim of gold; of hammered work you shall make them **at the two ends** of the mercy seat. Make one cherub **at one end**, and the other cherub **at the other end**; you shall make the cherubim **at the two ends** of it of one piece with the mercy seat. And the cherubim shall stretch out their wings above, covering the*

*mercy seat with their wings, **and they shall face one
another**; the faces of the cherubim shall be toward the
mercy seat.*

Many commentators have spotted the similarity. B.F.
Westcott noted more than one hundred years ago that the
scene in John 20:12 was 'like the cherubim on the mercy-
seat, between which "the Lord of hosts dwelt"'.[12] In his
devotional commentary William Temple wrote, 'The
place of his burial was between two angels; for God had
set Him forth in his blood to be a mercy-seat – the place
where God's forgiveness meets man's sin.'[13] Raymond
Brown said that the scene 'recalls the two cherubs on
either side of the Ark of the Covenant in the Holy of
Holies'.[14] In his recent commentary on John, Lincoln
reports

> Some have suggested that the two angels are meant
> to recall the two cherubim positioned to face each
> other at the two ends of the mercy seat on the ark of
> the covenant (cf. Exodus 25:17–22). This would
> mean that the divine presence had been between the
> two angels in the resurrected body and would fit
> with the evangelist's stress elsewhere on Jesus as the
> embodiment of the divine presence.[15]

From these brief observations it seems clear that the
narrator wants to remind the informed reader of the Holy
of Holies in the Tabernacle.


## The Command to Let Go

A third and final gap involves Jesus' command to Mary
Magdalene not to touch or hold on to him. John 20:17 reads

*Jesus said to her, 'Do not cling to Me, for I have not yet ascended to My Father; but go to My brethren and say to them, "I am ascending to My Father and your Father, and to My God and your God."'*

Once again we are confronted by 'gaps' in the narrator's showing and telling here. Why does Jesus seem so reluctant to have any kind of physical contact with Mary Magdalene? This question becomes even more acute when the context of this episode within John 20 is borne in mind. John 20 as a whole can be divided thus:

Introduction: 20:1–10:
- Jesus appears to Mary Magdalene (20:11–18)
- Jesus appears to the disciples (20:19–23)
- Jesus appears to Thomas (20:24–29)
Conclusion: 20:30–31

This structure suggests a series of notable contrasts between Mary Magdalene and Thomas:

| Mary Magdalene | Thomas |
|---|---|
| Female disciple | Male disciple |
| Outside, in a garden | Inside, behind closed doors |
| On Sunday, day one | On Sunday, day eight |
| Not one of the Twelve | One of the Twelve |
| First person to see risen Jesus in John 20 | Last person to see risen Jesus in John 20 |
| Not allowed to hold on to Jesus | Invited to touch Jesus' wounds |
| Confesses Jesus as Rabboni and Lord | Confesses Jesus as 'My Lord and my God' |

A very striking difference between these two characters is the fact that Jesus does not allow physical contact from Mary Magdalene whereas he does allow contact from Thomas. In John 20:26–27 the narrator reports

*And after eight days His disciples were again inside, and Thomas with them. Jesus came, the doors being shut, and stood in the midst, and said, 'Peace to you!' Then He said to Thomas, 'Reach your finger here, and look at My hands; and reach your hand here, and put it into My side. Do not be unbelieving, but believing.'*

Now this is very strange. Why is it that Mary Magdalene cannot touch Jesus on the first Easter morning, while Thomas is allowed to eight days later? What has changed between days one and eight to mean that Jesus is no longer untouchable?

Many solutions to this enigma have been proposed since the earliest days of the church.

Some have argued that Jesus' wounds were too sore and that they were not yet sufficiently healed on day one to be touched.

Others have argued that Jesus is concerned for Mary's purity. His body is still in some senses 'dead' until he has ascended to the Father. Mary must not be ritually defiled by touching what is dead.

Others have argued that Mary Magdalene was a woman with an immoral past while Thomas was a man who had not led such a life. Therefore he could touch Jesus while she could not.

Others have proposed that Jesus is in fact reprimanding Mary Magdalene, telling her to show more respect for his glorified body by not touching it. Thomas was allowed to touch Jesus' body because he was one of the twelve apostles. Mary Magdalene was not.

At least one scholar has suggested that Jesus was naked at this stage and that he was telling Mary Magdalene that touch was inappropriate until she too has gone to heaven after she has died.

Others have even suggested that Mary is being reprimanded for testing whether Jesus' body is physical or not.

All these and other theories have been proposed as a solution to Jesus' strange command not to cling to or touch Jesus. None of them is convincing. Some commentators, recognising this, have simply tried to cut the Gordian knot by suggesting that the original Greek manuscripts are wrong and that Jesus said something different from 'Stop touching me.' These vary from 'Touch me' (i.e. eliminating the negative, and therefore the problem) to 'Don't be afraid.' None of these textual emendations have found any kind of acceptance. The problem remains.

## A Time to Stoop Down

Like the empty tomb, the text of John 20:1–18 opens up as a portal for the energetic and enquiring. Here we stand, like Mary Magdalene, on the threshold of great discoveries that require us to see not only with our physical eyes but also with spiritual understanding. How are we to see – really see – what the narrator wants us to see? How are we to decode and decipher this encrypted text?

Before such great mysteries, it is important to stoop low in humility rather than stand in an attitude of pride. There is quite a lot of this 'stooping' in our text. In verse 5, we see the beloved disciple 'stooping down' in order to enter the tomb and discover its secrets. The narrator reports that 'he, stooping down and looking in, saw the linen cloths lying there'. The word translated 'stoop down' is the Greek verb *parakupto*. It is the same word that is used in verse 11 of Mary stooping down. There we read that 'as she wept she stooped down and looked into the tomb'. While this verb points quite simply to the way the tomb was cut into a rock like a cave, requiring the person to step down in order to enter, it also serves a metaphorical purpose. To enter the things of heaven we need to become small and keep low, as a child. Like Lewis Carroll's Alice, we must shut up like a telescope and become small so that we can enter through the door into a garden landscape that will cause us to wonder.

Stooping low is therefore an important key. The beloved disciple stoops low and looks into the tomb. So does Mary Magdalene. So does Peter, according to Luke 24:12. All of these followers of Jesus enter into a deeper understanding of Easter. This is a lesson for the reader. If we are to discover the riches in these verses we must approach the text with the right posture – the *parakupto* posture.

The word *parakupto* is used in two other passages in the New Testament which have something to say to us about our attitude as readers. One is 1 Peter 1:10–12:

> *Of this salvation the prophets have inquired and searched carefully, who prophesied of the grace that would come to you, searching what, or what manner of time, the Spirit of Christ who was in them was indicating when He testified beforehand the sufferings of Christ and the glories that would follow. To them it was revealed that, not to themselves, but to us they were ministering the things which now have been reported to you through those who have preached the gospel to you by the Holy Spirit sent from heaven – things which angels desire to look into.*

That last comment is very noteworthy. Peter has been

talking about how the Old Testament prophets spoke by revelation of the things to come, particularly the suffering and the glory of Jesus Christ (i.e. his death and resurrection). They themselves did not see with their own eyes what they were speaking about, but Peter has, and now Peter proclaims these truths with the help of the Holy Spirit. And these truths are things which angels long to stoop down and see (*parakupto*). What a thought that is! We have revelation that even heavenly beings long to observe! As the NIV puts it, 'Even angels long to look into these things.'

The second passage is James 1:25. In James 1:21–25 the author exhorts his readers to live holy lives – lives in obedience to God's Word:

> *Therefore lay aside all filthiness and overflow of wickedness, and receive with meekness the implanted word, which is able to save your souls. But be doers of the word, and not hearers only, deceiving yourselves. For if anyone is a hearer of the word and not a doer, he is like a man observing his natural face in a mirror; for he observes himself, goes away, and immediately forgets what kind of man he was. But he who looks into the perfect law of liberty and continues in it, and is not a forgetful hearer but a doer of the work, this one will be blessed in what he does.*

Notice the comment about 'looking into the perfect law of liberty'. Here again we have the verb *parakupto*. Reading God's Word in an obedient way requires that we stoop low and study hard. As the NLT puts it,

> *If you keep looking steadily into God's perfect law – the law that sets you free – and if you do what it says and don't forget what you heard, then God will bless you for doing it.*

## Reading in the Right Way

Stooping low is therefore very important if we are to discover the secrets of John 20:1–18. There really are mysteries here. Why does the narrator go to the trouble of being so precise about the grave clothes? Why does the narrator make such a point of describing the exact posture of the angels in the tomb – one at each end of the place where Jesus' body had been lying? Why does Jesus tell Mary Magdalene she cannot have physical contact with him, while within a few verses of the same chapter he encourages Thomas to touch him?

If we are to mind and fill these gaps there are some critical principles for our reading.

First of all, we need to read with an attitude of dependency on the Holy Spirit. It is one of the foundational beliefs of Christians that the Bible is inspired by the Holy Spirit. While debates continue about the exact nature of this inspiration, and indeed the kind of authority that the Bible possesses, this much is agreed by most: the Bible is great literature but it is also more than that. It is literature which God has breathed into by his Spirit. As such, the faithful reading of the Bible requires faith in what John Wesley called 'double inspiration'. In other words, the same Holy Spirit who inspired the authors of these texts is required by the reader for their illumination. Without the Holy Spirit we may understand the historical and linguistic realities of a text but we will not unearth the revelatory riches there. We simply cannot do without the Holy Spirit. Our reading must be a reading enlightened by the Spirit of God if it is to yield the treasures hidden and waiting for us.

Secondly, we need to make sure that our reading is consistent with the original meaning of the words in their context. In other words, we must be specific about what John actually meant by 'the grave clothes', 'the two angels' and Jesus' command to stop holding on to him. We must ensure that any proposal about the significance of these words is consistent with their original meaning, discerned with the tried and tested tools of historical, literary and linguistic analysis. Whatever reading we come up with, it must be in alignment with the meaning of the words as we have them.

Thirdly, we must also make sure that the answer proposed is consistent with the author's way of thinking, as exhibited throughout the rest of the fourth gospel. In other words, we cannot come up with a theory about the grave clothes, the angels and the prohibition of contact which is out of sync with the way the author is seen to think throughout the rest of the gospel. It must be related to other themes in the fourth gospel as a whole.

Fourthly, one thing we do know about the author of John's gospel is that he was someone who interpreted the life of Jesus in the light of the Old Testament and specifically the Jewish festivals celebrated in the Temple. Whatever solution is proposed for the three details we are highlighting here, it needs to be consistent with Jewish and specifically Old Testament thought patterns. Comparisons from other religious or philosophical backgrounds should not be used as the primary interpretative background, even if they provide some useful parallels. The Jewish background should be our first port of call. John's gospel is a thoroughly Jewish gospel written for a predominantly Jewish Christian community.

Fifthly, our interpretative reading of John 20:1–18 should as far as possible embrace all three details. If a solution can be found that explains the symbolic significance of all three codes (the grave clothes, the angels and the prohibition of touch), so much the better.

Finally, the proposal should be consistent with John's portrayal of Jesus and indeed cast greater light on his

# 70    *The Resurrection Code*

understanding of the person and work of Jesus Christ. The reading should open up greater faith and understanding of the one who conquered death and rose from the grave. It should open the door to a richer understanding of the meaning and significance of the resurrection of Jesus Christ.

These are the critical features of the reading offered here.

## The Angels Hold the Key

It is my conviction that John 20:1–18 is written in an encoded way. The gaps in information and explanation are the clue to this. There is something about Mary in this passage. And there is something about Jesus too. A superficial reading misses the significance of both. But a rereading yields the distinct impression that – as in Wordsworth's Lucy poem – there is far more than meets the eye. Something is going on here and we stand at the edge of it, like Mary at the tomb, peering in with eager eyes. But what is it?

It is my view that the key that unlocks the whole passage is in the narrator's intriguing description of the two angels, one at each end of the place where Jesus' body had been placed. This is so obviously significant we would be foolish to miss it. It is as if the narrator has frozen the two angels in time, captured as if posing for a Renaissance artist. It is a carefully and self-evidently choreographed description and, as such, calls out for attention from the reader. So what is the narrator saying?

A number of commentators – especially in the British tradition of commentaries on John – have noticed in passing that the angels seem to be positioned like the cherubim over the mercy seat of the Ark of the Covenant in Moses' Tabernacle.

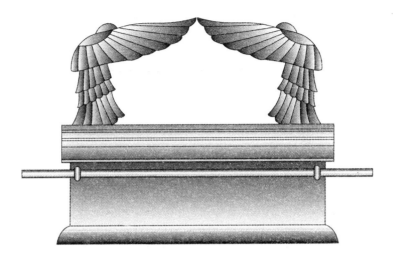

Commentators never make any more of this, other than noting the similarities between the angels in John 20:12 and the angels over the mercy seat. But I believe that these passing references to the cherubim are vital for unlocking the Resurrection Code in John 20:1–18. The angels hold the key to the mysterious Easter enigma in John's account of the encounter between Mary Magdalene and the risen Jesus. In itself it is the most wonderful story. As British scholar C.H. Dodd remarked,

> I cannot rid myself of the feeling . . . that this pericope has something indefinably first-hand about it. It stands in any case alone. There is nothing quite like it in the gospels. Is there anything quite like it in ancient literature?[16]

On the face of it, the story tells a most poignant tale of a grieving woman discovering that the one whom she thought was dead is in fact alive. Anyone who has been bereaved will feel the poignant and emotive power of such a story. But beyond this there is a sense that the text is tying to tell us something, beckoning us beyond its surface to the depths. Like Wordsworth's poem, the gaps in the text open up a sense of a 'multi-story' or multi-layered dynamism in the narration. It is my belief that the angels of John 20:12 hold the key. Once we have identified this key we can unlock the secrets of the text. And this process of unlocking will lead to discoveries that cause us to wonder and to worship. And in the end we may be led to proclaim

Thine be the glory, risen, conquering Son;
endless is the victory, thou o'er death hast won;
angels in bright raiment rolled the stone away,
kept the folded grave clothes where thy body lay.

Words: E.L. Budry

*Who has ascended into heaven, or descended?*
*Who has gathered the wind in His fists?*
*Who has bound the waters in a garment?*
*Who has established all the ends of the earth?*
*What is His name, and what is His Son's name,*
*If you know?*

Proverbs 30:4

# 4

# Into the Holy of Holies

The poet John Milton once wrote that 'millions of spiritual creatures walk the earth unseen, both when we wake and when we sleep'. With all the talk about the godless and atheistic materialism of the Western world, you would think that interest in such 'spiritual creatures' would have all but disappeared. But the opposite is the case. There is intense preoccupation with such beings, particularly angels.

People today are fascinated with angels, whether they are followers of a particular religion or not. Study the shelves in any Body, Mind, Spirit section of a bookstore and you will see many titles about the existence and role of angels. For all the claims that our culture is secular, this and many other signs point to a deep longing within our society for a transcendent reality and meaning. The preoccupation with angelic beings is a clear indication that we are not willing to let go of the spiritual dimension of life without a fight. To quote Peter Berger's famous book title, there are 'rumours of angels' everywhere – in popular music, movies, novels, TV series, computer games and many other places. As Emily Dickinson put it,

74

We trust, in plumed procession,
For such the angels go,
Rank after rank, with even feet
And uniforms of snow.

Emily Dickinson 'To fight Aloud is Very Brave'

It is common enough to see statues of angels at the site of tombs today. Two angels were present the first Easter morning at the tomb where Jesus' body had been placed. All four New Testament gospels report their presence at the site of Jesus' burial, although, coming as they do from different historical traditions, they vary on whether one was seen or two. They also vary in what the angels say to the women present at the tomb. While Mark, Matthew and Luke have the angels announcing the news of the resurrection, John depicts them sitting in the tomb and asking one simple question of Mary. And while in Mark, Matthew and Luke their message is expressed by proclamation, in John it is conveyed by posture.

In Mark, Matthew and Luke, their role is to announce the news that Jesus is alive. In Matthew's version the details in the angel's message are very specific. Matthew 28:5–7 reads

*The angel answered and said to the women, 'Do not be afraid, for I know that you seek Jesus who was crucified. He is not here; for He is risen, as He said. Come, see the place where the Lord lay. And go quickly and tell His disciples that He is risen from the dead, and indeed He is going before you into Galilee; there you will see Him. Behold, I have told you.'*

Mark 16:6–7 is very similar, as is Luke 24:5–7. In John's account the situation is very different. The angels do not announce the news of Jesus' resurrection. That role is given to Jesus himself. He is the one who tells Mary that he is ascending to the Father and that she is to go and tell the disciples. In John the role of the angels seems to be much more related to what they are doing rather than what they are saying. Indeed, in John's version the only words uttered by the angels are, 'Woman, why are you weeping?' They ask this question from within the tomb, in their very deliberate position at each end of the place where Jesus' body had been lying.

The differences between the other gospel reports and the one found in John reveal that there is indeed something very intriguing about the angels of John 20 verse 12. They cry out for attention. What is the signal they are sending? This is an important question because, as Linda Solegato once said, 'Angels are messengers, but sometimes we misunderstand their language.' What message are John's rather quiet angels communicating?

We saw in the last chapter that the most compelling suggestion is that the two angels in John 20:12 are meant to remind us of the cherubim in the Holy of Holies in the Tabernacle of Moses. Scholars have noticed this before and mentioned it, but only in passing. My conviction is that these angels are the key that unlocks the secrets of the entire episode. Much of John 20:1–18 is dependent on Old Testament ideas connected with the Tabernacle. If we do not discern the inter-textual echoes with the Old Testament we will miss the point. The angels point the way, but then they so often do. As Thomas Aquinas put it in his *Summa Theologica*, 'We are like children, who stand in need of masters to enlighten us and direct us; God has provided for this, by appointing his angels to be our teachers and guides.' The angels blaze the trail for us. Their presence and their position in the tomb is the message, and the message is this: 'Look to the Holy of

Holies. Look to the Tabernacle of Moses. There you will find the key to the Easter Enigma.'

## The Tabernacle of Moses

In the days of Moses, the Tabernacle was the place where God was said to dwell. The word 'tabernacle' means 'tent' and refers to the portable structure set up during the wilderness wanderings of the people of Israel. God had been very precise with his instructions for the Tabernacle. He gave the blueprints in Exodus chapters 25 – 31; the people actually built the Tabernacle in Exodus chapters 35 – 40.

At Mount Sinai the Lord told Moses about the materials and the measurements to use, as well as the overall design of the Tabernacle. There was to be an outer court with a bronze altar for sacrifices and a bronze urn for ritual washing. There was to be a sanctuary or holy place containing a seven-branched golden lampstand (known as the *menorah*), a golden table containing showbread, and a golden altar of incense. At the end of the sanctuary there was to be a much smaller chamber known as the Holy of Holies. This was to be separated from the Holy Place by an ornate veil with an artistic representation of the cherubim. In the Holy of Holies, or the Most Holy Place as it was also called, the Ark of the Covenant (also referred to as the Ark of the Testimony) was kept. It was overlaid with the covering known as the mercy seat, which – as we saw at the end of the last chapter – had two angels or cherubim, one at each end. Inside the Ark were the stone tablets of the Ten Commandments given by God to Moses on Mount Sinai. Overall, the layout looked like this:

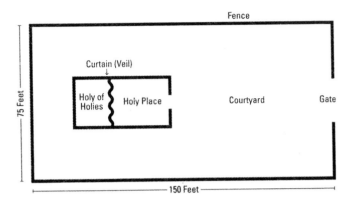

The Tabernacle was referred to by the word *mishkan* in Hebrew, meaning 'tent', 'dwelling' or 'habitation'. It was the place where the *shekinah* of God dwelt. *Shekinah* is the Hebrew for God's glory. God's glorious presence was said to reside in the Most Holy Place. The Tabernacle was carried everywhere by the people of Israel. When the presence of God moved, the people moved the Tabernacle until the Presence rested again. 'Whenever the cloud was taken up from above the tabernacle, the children of Israel would go onward in all their journeys' (Ex. 40:36).

The Tabernacle was consequently a place of great holiness. There were strict regulations about who was allowed to enter and at what times of the year. Only the high priest was allowed to go beyond the veil into the Holy of Holies, and then only once a year on the Day of Atonement. God chose Aaron and his descendants to be the first people to serve as priests before him in the Tabernacle. They were required to wear garments and various insignia that again were designed by the Lord. Elaborate rituals of cleansing were required for the priests before they could serve the Lord in the Tabernacle. The priests were then consecrated to their tasks, which

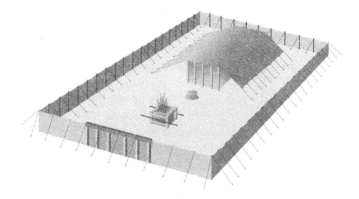

included offering sacrifices on the bronze altar, replenishing the showbread in the sanctuary, and keeping the lampstand tended and constantly burning.

The Tabernacle remained the meeting place between God and humanity until the time of the Temple (in Solomon's reign). The design and the furnishings of the Temple were the same as for the Tabernacle.

## One Greater than Moses

Right from the beginning of John's gospel there are references to Moses, the Exodus and the Tabernacle. In the prologue of the fourth gospel, the narrator gives us a magnificent insight into the identity and purpose of Jesus the Messiah. In John 1:14 he announces

*And the Word became flesh and dwelt among us, and we beheld His glory, the glory as of the only begotten of the Father, full of grace and truth.*

The word translated 'dwelt among us' is the Greek verb *skenein* which means 'to pitch a tent'. This is an allusion to

*The Resurrection Code*

the Tabernacle of Moses. Indeed, the memory of Moses is picked up a few verses later in John's prologue, in John 1:17, which is one of thirteen references to Moses in John's gospel (New Revised Standard Version):

| | |
|---|---|
| John 1:17 | The law indeed was given through **Moses**; grace and truth came through Jesus Christ. |
| John 1:45 | Philip found Nathanael and said to him, 'We have found him about whom **Moses** in the law and also the prophets wrote, Jesus son of Joseph from Nazareth.' |
| John 3:14 | And just as **Moses** lifted up the serpent in the wilderness, so must the Son of Man be lifted up. |
| John 5:45–46 | Do not think that I will accuse you before the Father; your accuser is **Moses**, on whom you have set your hope. If you believed **Moses**, you would believe me, for he wrote about me. |
| John 6:32 | Then Jesus said to them, 'Very truly, I tell you, it was not **Moses** who gave you the bread from heaven, but it is my Father who gives you the true bread from heaven.' |
| John 7:19 | Did not **Moses** give you the law? Yet none of you keeps the law. Why are you looking for an opportunity to kill me? |
| John 7:22–23 | **Moses** gave you circumcision (it is, of course, not from **Moses**, but from the patriarchs), and you circumcise a man on the sabbath. If a man receives circumcision on the sabbath in order that the law of **Moses** may not be broken, are you angry with me because I healed a man's whole body on the sabbath? |
| John 8:5 | Now in the law **Moses** commanded us to stone such women. Now what do you say? |
| John 9:28–29 | Then they reviled him, saying, 'You are his disciple, but we are disciples of **Moses**. We know that God has spoken to **Moses**, but as for this man, we do not know where he comes from.' |

No other Old Testament character receives as much attention in John's gospel as Moses does. Jesus is compared with Moses time and time again and the message is this: Jesus is one greater than Moses who leads his people on an Exodus out of slavery to sin. This was very much in line with the prophetic expectation expressed in Deuteronomy 18:15–19:

> 'The LORD your God will raise up for you a Prophet like me from your midst, from your brethren. Him you shall hear, according to all you desired of the LORD your God in Horeb in the day of the assembly, saying, "Let me not hear again the voice of the LORD my God, nor let me see this great fire anymore, lest I die." And the LORD said to me: "What they have spoken is good. I will raise up for them a Prophet like you from among their brethren, and will put My words in His mouth, and He shall speak to them all that I command Him. And it shall be that whoever will not hear My words, which He speaks in My name, I will require it of him."'

In John's gospel, Jesus is the fulfilment of this Messianic prophecy. He is the prophet like Moses and of course more than just a prophet. He is the divine 'I Am' on earth. He is the human habitation of the *shekinah* glory of God.

## One Greater than the Tabernacle

You cannot escape the inter-textual echoes with Moses, the Exodus and the Tabernacle in the gospel of John. The Tabernacle is especially important in relation to the plot of the gospel. The journey of Jesus throughout John is described in ways that remind the informed reader of the journey undertaken by the ancient priests through the Tabernacle.

The Tabernacle was composed of three main sections: the outer court, the sanctuary and the Holy of Holies. There were seven main items of furniture in these three parts of the Tabernacle:

1 The bronze altar of sacrifice
2 The bronze urn of water
3 The golden table of showbread
4 The golden menorah or lampstand
5 The golden altar of incense
6 The Ark of the Covenant
7 The mercy seat and the cherubim

John's gospel begins with the prologue (Jn. 1:1–18), in which Jesus is described as 'tabernacling with us' (Jn. 1:14) (my own translation). This echoes the Tabernacle of Moses in the Book of Exodus.

The first place where the priests of old would stop was the bronze altar of sacrifice. Here specific offerings were made as a sacrifice for sin. It is no surprise then to find allusions to sacrifice in the early chapters of John's gospel. In John 1:29 and 1:36 John the Baptist declares that Jesus is the Lamb of God who takes away the sin of the world. Jesus, in other words, is the fulfilment of the Passover sacrifices. Then there are the key words about the Cross in John 3:13–15:

*No one has ascended to heaven but He who came down from heaven, that is, the Son of Man who is in heaven. And as Moses lifted up the serpent in the wilderness, even so must the Son of Man be lifted up, that whoever believes in Him should not perish but have eternal life.*

Here a clear note of sacrifice is struck very early in the gospel.

The second place where the priests of old would stop was the bronze urn of water. Here they would wash before entering the sanctuary. Water was therefore vital in the Tabernacle and the ministry of the priests. And it is vital in John's gospel. Indeed, there is a lot of water in John's story:

*Jesus said to them, 'Fill the waterpots with water.' (Jn. 2:7)*

*Jesus answered, 'Most assuredly, I say to you, unless one is born of water and the Spirit, he cannot enter the kingdom of God.' (Jn. 3:5)*

*'Whoever drinks of this water will thirst again, but whoever drinks of the water that I shall give him will never thirst. But the water that I shall give him will become in him a fountain of water springing up into everlasting life.' (Jn. 4:13–14)*

*On the last day, that great day of the feast, Jesus stood and cried out, saying, 'If anyone thirsts, let him come to Me and drink. He who believes in Me, as the Scripture has said, out of his heart will flow rivers of living water.' (Jn. 7:37–38)*

The third place where the priests would minister was in the sanctuary, at the table of showbread. The showbread was a reminder of God's provision of manna during the wilderness wanderings in the book of Exodus. It should not therefore surprise us to find a great deal of material on the theme of bread in John's gospel, especially in chapter 6. After the feeding of the five thousand (involving bread, of course), Jesus crosses the lake. The people follow and a great debate ensues about bread.

This begins in verses 30–33:

> *Therefore they said to Him, 'What sign will You perform then, that we may see it and believe You? What work will You do? Our fathers ate the manna in the desert; as it is written, "He gave them bread from heaven to eat."' Then Jesus said to them, 'Most assuredly, I say to you, Moses did not give you the bread from heaven, but My Father gives you the true bread from heaven. For the bread of God is He who comes down from heaven and gives life to the world.'*

This leads to the climactic saying in John 6:35:

> *Jesus said to them, 'I am the bread of life. He who comes to Me shall never hunger, and he who believes in Me shall never thirst.'*

Throughout John 6 there are strong echoes of the story of Moses and the wilderness journey after the Exodus. Jesus presents himself not only as the true sacrifice and the living water but also as the true bread of life. Jesus fulfils all that was symbolised in the table of showbread, as he makes clear in John 6:49–51:

> *Your fathers ate the manna in the wilderness, and are dead. This is the bread which comes down from heaven, that one may eat of it and not die. I am the living bread which came down from heaven. If anyone eats of this bread, he will live forever; and the bread that I shall give is My flesh, which I shall give for the life of the world.*

The next port of call for the ancient priests was the seven-branched golden lampstand known as the menorah. The priest's task was to keep the fire burning and the lights shining. It is interesting therefore to note John 8:12:

*Then Jesus spoke to them again, saying, 'I am the light of the world. He who follows Me shall not walk in darkness, but have the light of life.'*

This statement was uttered during the Feast of Tabernacles in Jerusalem. Jesus is the fulfilment of the longing for light, embodied by the golden menorah in the Tabernacle of old. In Jesus, the hope of illumination and purification is found. As Jesus says in John 9:4–5,

*'I must work the works of Him who sent Me while it is day; the night is coming when no one can work. As long as I am in the world, I am the light of the world.'*

After tending the golden lampstand, the priest would move to the golden altar of incense that stood before the veil separating the Holy from the Most Holy Place. This was where the priest paused and made intercession for the people of God. This is precisely what we find Jesus doing in the climactic section of the Farewell Discourses in John chapters 13 – 17. John 17 in its entirety is a prayer by Jesus to the Father on behalf of his people. From the earliest days of the church this has been referred to as 'the High Priestly prayer of Jesus'. Cyril of Alexandria put it beautifully: 'Since he is the High Priest of our souls . . . he most fittingly makes prayer on our behalf.' The high priest on the Day of Atonement pronounced the 'name' of God ten times. In John 17 Jesus, in his High Priestly prayer, tells the Father that he has declared to his disciples 'your name'.

Then there is the crucifixion of Jesus in John 19. The seamless garment worn by Jesus on the Cross is very significant. In John 19:23 the narrator reports:

*Then the soldiers, when they had crucified Jesus, took His garments and made four parts, to each soldier a part, and*

> *also the tunic. Now the tunic was without seam, woven from the top in one piece.*

This has been compared to the seamless tunic worn by the high priest on the Day of Atonement. The word John uses is *chiton*, which is the same as the word used for Aaron's garment in the Greek translation of Leviticus 16 verse 4. In addition we have the advantage of the description of the high priest's garment given by the Jewish historian Josephus in his book *Antiquities of the Jews*:

> Now this tunic was not composed of two pieces nor was it sewn together upon the shoulders and the sides, but it was one long garment so woven as to have an opening for the neck. (III.VII.4)

Putting all this together, there is a broad structural similarity between the journey of the priest through the Tabernacle and the journey of Jesus throughout the story of John's gospel. It is almost as if the structure of the gospel and the structure of the Tabernacle are one and the same. Jesus fulfils the symbolism of the Tabernacle and its ministrations. He is the fulfilment of all the sacrifices of the Tabernacle (and later, the Temple too). He is the fulfilment of the longings expressed through the water of cleansing, the showbread and the lampstand. He is the one who is the true intercessor, standing and praying on our behalf to the Father. He is not only the priest but also the victim, the one sacrificed for the sin of the world.

Jesus makes a journey through John's story that looks like the journey of the high priest from the outer gate of the Tabernacle to the very edge of the Holy of Holies:

| The Tabernacle | John's story of Jesus |
|---|---|
| Bronze altar of sacrifice | John 3:14–15, Jesus lifted up as Moses lifted the bronze serpent |

| | |
|---|---|
| Bronze laver of water | John 3:5, 'You must be born of water and the Spirit.' |
| | John 4:13–14, the living water |
| The table of showbread | John 6:35, 'I am the bread of life.' |
| The golden lampstand | John 8:12, 9:4–5, 'I am the light of the world.' |
| The altar of incense | John 17, the High Priestly Prayer, v.9, 'I pray for them.' |

The only question that remains is this: where is the Holy of Holies in John's gospel? Where is the mercy seat?

## The Day of Atonement

The angels in John 20:12 are the clue. The two angels situated at either side of the stone where Jesus' body had been lying provide us with an important lead. Their presence suggests that the empty tomb has become the Holy of Holies and the angels are the equivalent of the cherubim at the mercy seat. The angels are therefore a key to unlocking John's 'resurrection code'. They are the ones who – with almost complete silence – send the reader a critical message.

In order to understand the message we must go back to the Tabernacle once again, and particularly to the occasion each year on which the high priest was permitted to go through all the parts of the Tabernacle, including the Most Holy Place. I am referring to the Day of Atonement, known also as *Yom Kippur*.

What, then, did the high priest do on that day? We learn about the rituals of the Day of Atonement from Leviticus chapter 16. In summary, the day's events went like this. Once a year the high priest – known in Hebrew as *cohen ha'gadol* – prepared himself carefully for the Day of Atonement, which took place during the autumn. On the day itself he would wash his whole body before removing his clothes and putting on his sacred garments. He presented a young bull to the Lord and brought two goats to the entrance of the Tabernacle, casting lots to see which would be killed and which would be sent out into the wilderness as a scapegoat. After that, he sacrificed the young bull as an atonement for his own sins and the sins of his family. He would take the blood of the bull into the Holy of Holies and sprinkle it in front of the atonement cover and against the front of the Ark. Then the goat would be slaughtered and its blood sprinkled in the same way as the bull's. This would make an atonement for the Holy of Holies and for the entire Tabernacle. Thereafter the high priest would take the bull's blood and smear it on the horns of the altar of sacrifice in the outer court, cleansing it from all defilement. After making atonement for the Ark, the Holy of Holies, the Tabernacle and the altar of sacrifice, the high priest would take the remaining living goat, lay his hands upon it and confess the sins of the whole people. Then he would send the goat into the wilderness. The high priest would then re-enter the Tabernacle and remove the garments he had been wearing for the Atonement ministrations. He would bathe before putting on new garments and offering a final sacrifice, making an atonement for himself and all of God's people. The remains of the animals used in the sacrifices would then be carried outside the camp and burned. Leviticus 16 concludes with a clear call to continue these practices throughout subsequent generations:

> *In future generations, the atonement ceremony will be performed by the anointed high priest who serves in place of his ancestor Aaron. He will put on the holy linen garments and make atonement for the Most Holy Place, the Tabernacle, the altar, the priests, and the entire*

*community. This is a permanent law for you, to make atonement for the Israelites once each year. (Lev. 16: 32–34, NLT)*

It is important at this point to remember that one of the unique features of John's gospel is its interest in the Feasts of the Lord mentioned in Leviticus 23. There were seven feasts in all:

1  Passover (*Pesach*)
2  Unleavened Bread (*Matzoh*)
3  First Fruits (*B'Korrim*)
4  Weeks/Pentecost (*Shavu'ot*)
5  Trumpets (*Rosh HaShannah*)
6  Day of Atonement (*Yom Kippur*)
7  Tabernacles (*Sukkot*)

The first four festivals are spring festivals (April, May), the second three autumn festivals (September/October).

In John's gospel, Jesus is portrayed as a faithful Jewish rabbi who attended the festivals of Judaism. Not all of the seven feasts are mentioned. John focuses especially on Passover (Jn. 2:13, 23; 6:4; 11:55; 12:1; 13:1; 18:28; 18:39; 19:14) and Tabernacles (7:2). He also includes an unnamed festival in John 4:45 and the Feast of Dedication or *Hanukkah* in John 10:22 – a festival not listed in the Old Testament but added in the second century BC. In John's gospel Jesus is portrayed not only attending the Feasts of the Lord, but also fulfilling them. Thus, Jesus fulfils the feast of Pesach or Passover by himself becoming the Passover Lamb. In John's gospel, the death of Jesus happens at the moment when the lambs are being slaughtered in the Temple on the Day of Preparation. His death is intentionally described in ways reminiscent of the death of these one-year-old male and unblemished lambs. So we find in John 19:31–33

*Therefore, because it was the Preparation Day, that the bodies should not remain on the cross on the Sabbath (for that Sabbath was a high day), the Jews asked Pilate that their legs might be broken, and that they might be taken away. Then the soldiers came and broke the legs of the first and of the other who was crucified with Him. But when they came to Jesus and saw that He was already dead, they did not break His legs.*

A few verses later the narrator points to the fulfilment motif in this action by saying in verse 36

*These things were done that the Scripture should be fulfilled, 'Not one of His bones shall be broken.'*

The reference here is to the regulations concerning the first Passover lambs in Exodus 12:46:

*In one house it shall be eaten; you shall not carry any of the flesh outside the house, nor shall you break one of its bones.*

Jesus in John's gospel is therefore presented to the informed reader as one who fulfils the Feasts of the Lord. This then leads us to the critical question in relation to this present study. If the angels in the tomb are reminiscent of the cherubim in the Most Holy Place, is this a message that Jesus fulfils the high priestly ministry of the Day of Atonement? Is the resurrection code concealed within John 20:1–18 a code to do with Jesus ascending into the most holy place in the realms of heaven? Does the reason behind Jesus' prohibition of physical contact have something to do with the transformation in the relationship between Jesus and his disciples from this moment on? Is Mary Magdalene in some senses a witness of this momentous and history-making transition? Is she in some sense or other a privileged interpreter of the Resurrection?

## Back to the Grave Clothes

The answer, I believe, is yes. So much of the mystery in John 20:1–18 is explained once we become familiar with the Feast of *Yom Kippur* and with John's emphasis on the way Jesus fulfils the Feasts of the Lord. The grave clothes are a good example. The narrator reports that the grave clothes were left by Jesus in the tomb. The language is very precise. Jesus leaves the linen cloths that were wound around his body and his head cloth lying neatly nearby. Simon Peter sees these articles of clothing. In John 20:6–7 we read

> *He saw the linen cloths lying there, and the handkerchief that had been around His head, not lying with the linen cloths, but folded together in a place by itself.*

The beloved disciple then enters the tomb, sees these same sights, and then believes. What he believes in at this point is not stated.

If we allow for a moment that the presence of the angels in the tomb points to the Holy of Holies and to the Day of Atonement, might the same be true of the grave clothes? I have already pointed to the parallels between the seamless garment worn by Jesus at the Cross and the one-piece white garment worn by the high priest at *Yom Kippur*. Obviously Jesus is not still wearing this same garment because the Roman soldiers cast lots for it. But what if the narrator wants to set up an association between Jesus' clothing and that of the high priest for the scene here at the empty tomb? What if this is a tactic designed to create resonances between Jesus' grave clothes and the garments of the high priest at *Yom Kippur*?

The articles of clothing worn by the high priest for the *Yom Kippur* rituals were a simple white one-piece garment, a white turban on the head and a sash around the waist. These garments were to be put on before the rituals began. As Leviticus 16:4 (NLT) says:

> *Then he must wash his entire body and put on his linen tunic and the undergarments worn next to his body. He must tie the linen sash around his waist and put the linen turban on his head. These are his sacred garments.*

After the rituals were complete, these garments were to be removed. The key verse for this is Leviticus 16:23 (NLT):

> *As Aaron enters the Tabernacle, he must take off the linen garments he wore when he entered the Most Holy Place, and he must leave the garments there.*

Two things suggest that the description of the grave clothes in John 20 is influenced by the Levitical description of the high priest's garments. First of all, in John 20 the narrator makes a point of emphasising that Jesus wore both a linen cloth around his body and a turban-like head cloth. This is reminiscent of Leviticus 16:4 – a text which is really the only plausible background for the language in John 20:6–7. Secondly, the reference to the grave clothes being simply left by Jesus in the empty tomb is reminiscent of the high priest leaving his garments within the Tabernacle.

In case we think this is far-fetched we should consider the description of the ascended Jesus in Revelation chapter 1. The book of Revelation comes from the same community, possibly the same author, as John's gospel. Here is what John saw on the penal colony island of Patmos. He describes a vision of the ascended Jesus in Revelation 1:12–13. Notice what Jesus is said to be wearing in the heavenly realms:

> *Then I turned to see the voice that spoke with me. And having turned I saw seven golden lampstands, and in the midst of the seven lampstands One like the Son of Man, clothed with a garment down to the feet and girded about the chest with a golden band.*

The word used here for 'a garment down to the feet' is *poderes*. Exactly the same word is used in the Greek translation of the Old Testament (known as the Septuagint) when it describes the high priest's full-length tunic in Exodus 29:5. In heaven, John sees Jesus wearing the garments of the high priest associated with *Yom Kippur*. If John could make such a clear reference to the high priest's garments in Revelation 1:12–13, why should he not do the same in John 20:6–7? Even if we cannot allow that the same author is responsible for both, surely we must concede that the same community is.

There seems to be a connection therefore between Jesus' grave clothes and the white *kitel* or garment of the high priest. White garments are worn by Jewish people today during *Yom Kippur* (by the rabbi and the cantor in the synagogue, for example). They are often compared with burial shrouds – indeed, the white *kitel* is the robe in which the dead are buried. In fact, it is customary to wear white on *Yom Kippur*, to remind people of Isaiah 1:18:

> *'Come now, and let us reason together,'*
> *Says the Lord,*
> *'Though your sins are like scarlet,*

*They shall be as white as snow;*
*Though they are red like crimson,*
*They shall be as wool.'*

The grave clothes of Jesus point to Jesus' role as both High Priest and victim in the *Yom Kippur* rituals. They highlight the subtext of John 20:1–18, which is to show that the events of the first Easter morning are fulfilling the Day of Atonement.

## Noli Me Tangere

And this brings us to the command of Jesus, uttered to Mary Magdalene, that she was to desist from holding on to him. For the high priest, physical contact with any other person was absolutely prohibited on the Day of Atonement. In fact, the high priest went to elaborate lengths not to be touched by anyone else in the run-up to and the conducting of the *Yom Kippur* rituals. Leviticus 16:17 points to this need to refrain from all human contact:

> *There shall be no man in the tabernacle of meeting when he goes in to make atonement in the Holy Place, until he comes out, that he may make atonement for himself, for his household, and for all the assembly of Israel.*

The high priest was accordingly protected against being touched on the Day of Atonement.

Now let us return to John 20. What do we see? We find Mary Magdalene, just after Jesus' resurrection, meeting Jesus outside the tomb. She reaches out to embrace him but he tells her to stop holding on to him because he is ascending – going up – to the Father. Physical contact is not allowed at this point, even though it is allowed eight days later when the risen Jesus appears to Thomas. Then Jesus presents the wounds of his crucifixion to Thomas and invites him to reach out and touch them. What is going on here?

If the rituals of *Yom Kippur* lie in the background, we have to conclude that Jesus is still in the process of completing his atoning work at this point. We should remember that the crucifixion, resurrection and ascension are regarded as inseparable by John. In the fourth gospel, Jesus' elevation on the Cross, his rising from the dead and his ascension are all seen as connected aspects of his being 'lifted up'. This being the case, it is entirely consistent with the rest of the fourth gospel's theology to propose that Jesus is in some kind of intermediate state when he meets Mary Magdalene. Some scholars are nervous of such an interpretation. As Mary Rose D'Angelo says, 'Most commentators have been chary of explaining the command to Mary as implying that the encounter takes place while Jesus is in a transitional state between the resurrection and the ascension.'[17] However, Origen (c. AD 185–254) seems to have sensed that Jesus was in a process of continuing transformation at this point. He wrote that Jesus was in 'a holy and awesome process', pointing out that the state of Jesus when he meets Mary Magdalene is different from the state of Jesus when he meets Thomas (and indeed the disciples). British commentator Hoskyns saw this too: he wrote, 'The command that Mary should cease touching Him refers to the interim period between the Resurrection and the Ascension – and to this period only.'[18]

It seems therefore that Mary Magdalene's encounter with Jesus occurs at a critical moment while Jesus is returning to the Father to present the offering of his atoning sacrifice on the Cross. Jesus cannot allow physical contact with him at this point, just as the high priest – ascending to the Holy of Holies – could not allow it. Both Jesus and the high priest at *Yom Kippur* would be at pains to say the same thing: 'Don't touch me. I have not gone up to the sanctuary yet.'

## Ascending to the Heavens

Mary Magdalene, in the early hours of the first Easter Day, came upon the resurrected Christ at the point of his ascension to the Holy of Holies in heaven. Jesus told Mary Magdalene not to hold on to him. Why? Because he says, 'I *am* ascending to my Father.' Not 'I will ascend (in forty days' time),' but 'I *am* ascending.' What did Jesus mean by 'ascending'?

In the Old Testament, the word 'ascend' (*alah*) is used 888 times. On many occasions it is used of ascending the hill of the Lord in Jerusalem in order to worship God in the Temple. Psalm 122:3–4 is a good example:

> *Jerusalem is built*
> *As a city that is compact together,*
> *Where the tribes go up,*
> *The tribes of the* LORD,
> *To the Testimony of Israel,*
> *To give thanks to the name of the* LORD.

On other occasions it is used specifically of priests going up into the Temple precincts to offer sacrifices (2 Kgs. 23:9). On still other occasions, the word was used of 'offering up' burnt sacrifices in the Temple itself. This was true for both the Tabernacle and the Temple. Thus we read of the worship in the Tabernacle in Leviticus 14:20:

*And the priest shall offer [alah] the burnt offering and the
grain offering on the altar. So the priest shall make
atonement for him, and he shall be clean.*

In the Old Testament the word 'ascend' is therefore
intimately connected with going up to the Tabernacle or
the Temple and with the worship of God.

In John's gospel we find the same thing. The word
translated 'ascend' is the Greek verb *anabaino*. It is used
seventeen times. On four occasions it is used simply to
describe people climbing or going up into ships,
sheepfolds and the like. On five occasions it is used of
Jesus ascending or going up into the heavens (1:51, 3:13,
6:62, 20:17 (twice)). But on nine occasions it is used of
Jesus or other people going up to Jerusalem to worship
God at the Temple feasts (2:13, 5:1, 7:8 (twice), 7:10
(twice), 7:14, 11:55, 12:20). A typical example is John 2:13,
where the narrator tells us, 'The Passover of the Jews was
at hand, and Jesus went up to Jerusalem.'

When Jesus says to Mary Magdalene, 'I am ascending
to my Father,' he uses language associated with going up
to the house of the Lord to worship. This is priestly
language. Jesus says that he is going up to the Father and
he uses terminology suggestive of going up to the most
sacred place in the house of God. The place to which the
high priest made his ascent in Jerusalem was the mercy
seat between the cherubim. The place to which Jesus was
ascending when he met Mary Magdalene was the throne
room of heaven, where he was to present his sacrifice to
the Father. Jesus is accordingly the great High Priest here,
going up to the Father in the process of his crucifixion,
resurrection and ascension. The ascension of Jesus in
John's gospel is an inextricable part of this process. It
is the risen Lord's presentation of his wounds to the

Father.

If this is so, then Jesus was interacting with his Father in a way that we cannot easily describe, in a realm beyond conventional notions of time and space. We know from the rest of John 20 that the risen Lord was not restricted by time and space. Here are several examples. The first is from John 20:19 (NLT):

*That evening, on the first day of the week, the disciples were meeting behind locked doors because they were afraid of the Jewish leaders. Suddenly, Jesus was standing there among them!*

Whatever kind of body this is, it is clearly spiritual as well as physical. It can materialise anywhere and locked doors are no obstacle. A few verses later, in John 20:26–27, we find this:

*Eight days later the disciples were together again, and this time Thomas was with them. The doors were locked; but suddenly, as before, Jesus was standing among them. He said, 'Peace be with you.' Then he said to Thomas, 'Put your finger here and see my hands. Put your hand into the wound in my side. Don't be faithless any longer. Believe!'*

Yet again we see how this body is spiritual – it can appear anywhere. And yet this body is not a phantom or an illusion. The body of the risen Jesus is not an intangible ghost. His body is a body that can be touched.

That being the case, the risen Jesus transcends creaturely categories of time and space. In his resurrected, spiritual body he breaks out of the restrictions of time and space that we experience on the earth and enters into the unrestricted Godward side of reality. Before the

Father he makes his priestly offering of his own blood.

## Yom Kippur Fulfilled

So the resurrected Christ, on the first Easter Day, fulfils all the expectations of the high priest on the Day of Atonement! The New Testament writer to the Hebrews surely captures the essence of this. He explains that the ceremonies of the Day of Atonement are a pattern of the atoning work of Christ. In the letter to the Hebrews, Jesus is our High Priest, and his blood shed at Calvary is seen as symbolised in the blood of bulls and goats. As the high priest entered the Holy of Holies with the blood of his sacrificial victim, so Jesus entered heaven itself to appear before the Father on behalf of his people. The writer puts it thus in chapter 9 verses 11 and 12 (NLT):

> *Christ has now become the High Priest over all the good things that have come. He has entered that great, perfect sanctuary in heaven, not made by human hands and not part of this created world. Once for all time he took blood into that Most Holy Place, but not the blood of goats and calves. He took his own blood, and with it he secured our salvation for ever.*

What then of Luke's account of the ascension of Jesus Christ in Acts 1? If Jesus ascends on the first Easter Sunday morning, in what sense can he be said to ascend forty days later?

The answer is this. The ascension on Easter day was not for the disciples' benefit but for the Father's. Jesus went to the throne room in heaven to show his Father the wounds in his hands and side, the scars that demonstrated his sacrifice. In reality, Jesus probably had far more interaction of this kind with the Father than we realise, even in his earthly life. The prayer of John 17 demonstrates this. It is a very curious prayer indeed. At times Jesus speaks as if he is in heaven, not on earth. At other times he speaks as if future events are past. Clearly, Jesus interacted with his Father in the heavens in a mystical and mysterious way during his earthly life. This is also indicated by the statement in John 3:13, 'No one has ascended to heaven but He who came down from heaven, that is, the Son of Man who is in heaven.' Notice the past tense 'has ascended'. If John 3:13 is Jesus speaking (rather than the narrator), it shows that ascension was not a one-off experience for Jesus in his earthly life. As Raymond Brown says in his commentary on this verse, 'There is a strange timelessness or indifference to normal time sequence that must be reckoned with.'[19] If interaction was this possible while he was in his physical body, how much more possible was it in his resurrected, spiritual body!

The ascension on Easter Day was therefore for the Father's benefit. The ascension recorded by Luke in Acts chapter 1 is for the disciples' benefit. They need to know that the risen Jesus has now gone from among them and that the Holy Spirit is coming soon to empower them as witnesses. They need to see Jesus going if they are to experience the Spirit coming.

### There's Something about Mary

What does all this tell us about Mary Magdalene? To Mary is given a unique privilege. Peering into the empty tomb, she sees the two angels, one at each end, where Jesus' body had been left. These angels are positioned like the cherubim in the Most Holy Place of the Tabernacle of Moses, the place where the presence of God dwelt. Mary Magdalene is therefore given a startling vision – she sees that the empty tomb is the place where God's glory is revealed. The resurrection of Christ has heralded a new dawn, a new way of relating to God as Father. Mary Magdalene sees the secret of all secrets, a secret that the discarded, folded grave clothes only hint at. Through tear-soaked eyes she sees the cherubim in the tomb and encounters Jesus, who is – through the eternal Spirit – offering himself unblemished before God (Heb. 9:14).

In this regard, Mary Magdalene fulfils the role of witness. She is the first to see the risen Jesus. When she does, Jesus tells her to stop clinging on to his body. He now lives in a resurrected, Spirit-animated physicality. Everything has changed for him and everything has changed for those, like Miriam of Magdala, who call him 'Lord'. From now on, Jesus will not be known 'according to the flesh' (2 Cor. 5:16). Mary has to let go of this kind of relationship. From now on, Mary will not cling to Jesus but cling to the Father – the Father whom Jesus has been revealing all the way through John's gospel, the Father to whom Jesus is ascending. Now that Jesus has presented his atoning work in heaven, the way has been opened for Mary and all those who follow Jesus, then and now, to know the Father intimately. Thanks to the atonement, every disciple can worship the Father in spirit and in truth. Through the death of the Son and the animating work of the Spirit, those who call themselves disciples of Jesus can find the way to the Father, know the truth of the Father, and experience the life of the Father (Jn. 14:6). Everything has changed.

What an honour is given here to Mary Magdalene! I am sure that she was never the same again. From this day on, Mary was well aware that Jesus' shed blood was indeed the all-sufficient sacrifice for her sins. From now on, Mary

Magdalene knew that – in the beautiful words of Charitie Bancroft:

> Before the throne of God above
> I have a strong and perfect plea,
> A great High Priest whose name is Love,
> Who ever lives and pleads for me.

*You killed the author of life, but God raised him from the dead.*

Acts 3:15 (NIV)

# 5

# Searching the Source

One major question remains in this study. Who was responsible for the 'resurrection code' in John 20:1–18? Who was the author and what kind of person was he – or she?

Before the question is answered, we must attend to some issues of terminology. Throughout this book I have been referring to the figure of the narrator or the storyteller in John 20:1–18. The narrator is the person whose voice we can hear right from the start of the narrative:

> *On the first day of the week Mary Magdalene went to the tomb early, while it was still dark, and saw that the stone had been taken away from the tomb.*

The narrator tells the story not from a first-person but from a third-person point of view. Some of the narrative consists of *telling*. The opening of the passage just quoted has the narrator telling us about the time, the location, the lead character and an event. Other parts of the passage consist of *showing* rather than telling. In other words, the narrator steps into the background and shows the characters speaking. Verse 2 gives us a good example:

*Then she ran and came to Simon Peter, and to the other
disciple, whom Jesus loved, and said to them, 'They have
taken away the Lord out of the tomb, and we do not know
where they have laid Him.'*

Here the narrator moves from telling to showing. He
shows Mary Magdalene speaking to the two disciples.

One of the mistakes many readers make is to confuse
the narrator with the author. But the narrator and the
author are not necessarily the same. Narrators are
characters. They either stand in an external relationship
or an internal relationship to events. Narrators who have
an internal relationship participate in the story. External
narrators stand outside the action and comment on it. In
John 20:1–18 we have an external narrator. This storyteller stands outside the events and sees more than the
characters within the story see. This accounts for the
considerable amount of irony in the fourth gospel. On
many occasions the narrator's more privileged point of
view sets up a distance between what the reader
understands and what the characters within the story
understand. This is because the narrator's point of view
is an omniscient one in John's gospel. His perspective is
an unlimited, trustworthy one.

If the narrator is part of the narrative world, the author
and the reader are part of the real world. In other words,
the author is a real person in history who creates a story.
In this case, the author of John 20:1–18 is the person who
compiled the oral and written traditions about Jesus and
then created a coherent account of events. This coherent
account is told from a particular and distinctive point of
view, and this point of view is where the narrator comes
in. The author of John's gospel created a narrator or
storyteller who has a unique perspective on the events
told in the story. Through the use of this narrator – in

John's case a third-person, omniscient and reliable narrator – the author communicates his message to the reader. Now the reader is like the author – a person who occupies the real world. The original readers were the audience for whom the author was writing in the first century AD. Today's readers are those in the real world who read John's story.

The diagram below provides a simplified depiction of the way an author communicates with a reader through the use of a narrator:

So far in this book we have studied the characters within the narrative world of John 20:1–18. This has involved a close reading of the portrayal of Mary Magdalene and Jesus. This has been our focus and the majority of the book has been devoted to the encoded narration of this text. But now we must broaden the discussion and move from the narrative world to the real world, from narrative criticism to narrative biography. Now we must ask, 'Who was the author responsible for the resurrection code in John 20:1–18?' The author rather than the narrator must therefore now come under the spotlight.

## Enter the Beloved Disciple

At the source of the tradition behind John's gospel is an enigmatic figure known as 'the disciple whom Jesus loved'. This 'beloved disciple' is the eyewitness whose reminiscences are responsible for the gospel story as a whole. This is clear from the penultimate verse of the gospel, in John 21:24. Speaking about this person, the narrator says

> *This is the disciple who testifies of these things, and wrote these things; and we know that his testimony is true.*

In another similar passage, this time in John 19:35, the narrator tells us that the reports of what happened to Jesus at the moment of his death came from the beloved disciple:

> *And he who has seen has testified, and his testimony is true; and he knows that he is telling the truth, so that you may believe.*

Within the narrative world of the fourth gospel there is consequently a person who is explicitly described in terms of their testimony. This character is not referred to by name but rather with the exalted and affectionate epithet, 'the disciple whom Jesus loved'. He is said to 'testify' to the things described in the gospel and to have actually seen what he has testified to. Indeed, the narrator is adamant that 'his testimony is true'.

This witness terminology serves two purposes in the fourth gospel. First of all it contributes towards the legal drama that unfolds in the story. There is a great deal of legal language in John's gospel. This is because Jesus is portrayed as the Judge on trial – not just during his interrogations in John 18 – 19 but throughout the entire narrative. This witness terminology serves a thematic purpose. It is important in relation to the beloved disciple because it helps cast him in the role of a faithful witness in the courtroom drama of the gospel.

The second purpose of the witness terminology is to confirm that John's gospel has an eyewitness reporter as the source of its information about the words and works of Jesus. This is particularly important because the gospel of John differs in many respects from the other New Testament gospels. To cite just one example, much of the action in John's gospel occurs in the south, around Jerusalem and in Judea, whereas in the other three gospels it occurs mainly in the north, in Galilee (at least until the time of Jesus' passion in Jerusalem). It seems that the gospel of John comes from a source independent from the other three gospels. This being the case, it is important to have the reassurance of the gospel itself that there is a disciple whose eyewitness testimony has formed the bedrock of the traditions contained in this gospel.

Where do we find the beloved disciple in the unfolding plot of the fourth gospel? His first explicit appearance is in John 13, the night before Jesus died. Jesus is with his disciples in Jerusalem and he has just washed their feet. He mentions that one of them will betray him and the disciples are said to be perplexed. The narrator then introduces a character for the first time: the beloved disciple.

*Now there was leaning on Jesus' bosom one of His disciples, whom Jesus loved. Simon Peter therefore motioned to him to ask who it was of whom He spoke. (Jn. 13:23–24)*

As the time of Jesus' death in Jerusalem draws near, the beloved disciple makes his first appearance, reclining next to Jesus, with his head upon the Rabbi's chest. Close to Jesus' heart, he has special access to Jesus' words and acts as an intermediary for Peter. The betrayer is then identified as Judas Iscariot.

The second appearance of the beloved disciple occurs during the arrest of Jesus. We are still in Jerusalem and Jesus has been seized in the garden and taken to Annas' residence. The narrator tells us in John 18:15

*And Simon Peter followed Jesus, and so did another disciple. Now that disciple was known to the high priest, and went with Jesus into the courtyard of the high priest.*

The unidentified figure referred to as 'another disciple' is commonly regarded as the beloved disciple. This follower of Jesus often appears with Simon Peter, as the first reference in John 13:23 attests. Here the beloved disciple is seen again helping Simon Peter. This time he secures access for Peter into the grounds where Jesus is being questioned. The reason why he is able to do this is supplied by the narrator. The beloved disciple is known to the high priest – an intriguing detail to which we shall return in due course.

The third reference to the beloved disciple also occurs in the Jerusalem area, this time just outside the city at the site of the crucifixion. The beloved disciple is the only male disciple present at the scene of Jesus' death. He stands with four women, one of whom is the mother of

Jesus. As Jesus approaches death, he charges the beloved disciple to look after his mother in a touching scene described in John 19:25–27:

*Now there stood by the cross of Jesus His mother, and His mother's sister, Mary the wife of Clopas, and Mary Magdalene. When Jesus therefore saw His mother, and the disciple whom He loved standing by, He said to His mother, 'Woman, behold your son!' Then He said to the disciple, 'Behold your mother!' And from that hour that disciple took her to his own home.*

Here the dying Jesus effectively adopts the beloved disciple into his own family, describing him as his mother's son, and telling him that Mary is now his mother. Here a new family is created and the beloved disciple is said to take the mother of Jesus to his own home.

The next reference to the beloved disciple is in John 19:35, which we have already looked at. Jesus is now dead but his body is still on the Cross. A Roman soldier pierces his corpse with a lance and blood and water immediately flow from the wound in his side. This causes the narrator to interject that the beloved disciple witnessed this with his own eyes and that his testimony is trustworthy and true. Clearly the beloved disciple did not leave immediately after Jesus' words to him in verses 25–27. He quite understandably stayed with the mother of Jesus at the site of the crucifixion until Jesus had died.

The next scene involving the beloved disciple is one that by now we should be very familiar with. It is John 20:1–10. We are still in the precincts of Jerusalem, and Mary Magdalene has been to the tomb of Jesus in the early hours of the first day of the week and found it empty. She returns and reports this to Simon Peter and the beloved disciple. Notice once again the pairing of Simon Peter with the beloved disciple. They then run together to the empty tomb. The beloved disciple outruns Peter and arrives at the tomb first and is the first to see the contents of the burial chamber. Peter goes in, followed by the beloved disciple. The latter is said to see the grave clothes and to believe. Then, after a remark about both disciples not yet appreciating that Jesus had to be raised (according to Old Testament prophecy), they return home.

The penultimate reference to the beloved disciple occurs in John 21, when the risen Jesus appears on the shore of Lake Tiberias. Peter is out at sea fishing with six others, one of whom is the beloved disciple. When Jesus tells the disciples to cast their nets out on the right-hand side of the boat, the beloved disciple immediately recognises who is speaking. John 21:7 simply states

*Therefore that disciple whom Jesus loved said to Peter, 'It is the Lord!'*

Here the beloved disciple is once again seen in relation to Simon Peter. Just as he reached the tomb before Peter, so he reaches the right conclusion before Peter.

The final explicit reference to the beloved disciple occurs in John 21. After a poignant breakfast scene in which Jesus reinstates Simon Peter (after Peter's three denials of Jesus in John 18), Peter is told of his destiny. He is going to be bound and then walked to a place he does not want to go to. This is a haunting allusion to his martyrdom. Hearing this, Peter points to the beloved disciple and says, 'What about him?' Jesus replies, 'If I want him to remain until I return, what is that to you?' This comment fuels expectation among the 'brothers' that the beloved disciple will not in fact die. As the narrator indicates in verse 23,

*Then this saying went out among the brethren that this disciple would not die. Yet Jesus did not say to him that he would not die, but, 'If I will that he remain till I come, what is that to you?'*

The narrator then follows this with the statement already mentioned about the beloved disciple writing about these things and his testimony being known to be true.

Looked at overall, there are only seven clear references to the beloved disciple in John's gospel:

- John 13:23–25
- John 18:15–18
- John 19:25–27
- John 19:31–37
- John 20:1–10
- John 21:7
- John 21:20–25

One other passage is sometimes included in addition to these: John 1:35–39, which mentions two disciples, one of whom is not identified (the other is named as Andrew). Some scholars speculate that the anonymous disciple is the beloved disciple but the evidence for this is not especially convincing.

## The Faithful Witness

Three things need to be noted about the beloved disciple in John's gospel. The first has to do with 'precedence'. In every passage where the beloved disciple appears he takes precedence over Simon Peter. In the first passage, 13:23–25, Peter has to ask the beloved disciple to ask Jesus who the betrayer is. In John 18:15–17, Peter needs the beloved disciple's help to gain access to the courtyard of the residence where Jesus is being interrogated. In John 19:25–27, the beloved disciple is the only male disciple present at the site of the crucifixion; Peter is nowhere to be seen. In John 19:35 the same applies. In John 20:1–10, the beloved disciple outruns Peter to the empty tomb and is said to see and believe first. In John 21:7 he recognises the risen Jesus before Peter does. In John 21:20–25 Peter takes umbrage at the fact that Jesus has promised him a martyr's death while nothing has been said about the beloved disciple's future. In every case, the beloved disciple takes precedence over Peter. While it is too much of an exaggeration to say that Peter is portrayed negatively, it is not an exaggeration to say that the beloved disciple is presented positively. His role is clearly one of a faithful witness.

The second thing that is interesting about the beloved disciple is his quality of perception. He is not only a faithful witness; he is also a perceptive one. The beloved disciple sees what Peter and others do not see concerning Judas. He sees the blood and water at the Cross and understands the significance of Jesus' legs not being broken. He sees the grave clothes in the empty tomb and believes. He sees the risen Lord at the edge of the sea and recognises who he is. Perception – by which I mean spiritual insight – is a critical characteristic of the beloved disciple.

The third noteworthy feature has to do with precision. In almost every passage where the beloved disciple is mentioned there is a heightened precision in the narration. Take the following:

- John 13:23–26: the beloved disciple notices the detail of Jesus dipping the bread and giving it to Judas
- John 18:15–17: he notices details concerning the personnel and the charcoal fire burning in the courtyard

- John 19:25–27: he notices who is around the Cross and what they are doing and saying
- John 19:33–35: he notices that Jesus' legs were not broken and that blood and water flowed from his side
- John 20:6–8: he notices the grave clothes in the empty tomb and includes detailed description of them
- John 21:9: he notices the details surrounding Jesus' preparation of breakfast, including the charcoal fire
- John 21:11: he notices and records the exact number of fish caught (153)

One cannot help noticing that the precision of detail increases markedly when the beloved disciple is mentioned in the story. As Derek Tovey remarks in his book, *Narrative Art and Act in the Fourth Gospel*,

> At every point where the beloved disciple appears . . . the narrative includes items of close detail which suggest 'on the spot', eyewitness report.[20]

While a cynic might claim that these are merely 'reality effects' inserted into the narrative to create an illusion of historicity, it is significant that observational detail greatly increases wherever the beloved disciple figures in the story. As Richard Bauckham has said, 'These details do help to give readers the impression that the Gospel portrays the Beloved Disciple as an observant witness of what happened.'[21]

To sum up, the beloved disciple is portrayed as someone who takes precedence over Simon Peter, whose insight into Jesus' words and acts is perceptive and whose reminiscences are precise and detailed.

## The Man With No Name

Mention of Richard Bauckham brings us now to the question of the identity of the beloved disciple, a topic addressed in his masterly and acclaimed 2006 book *Jesus and the Eyewitnesses*. This study of eyewitness testimony looks at all four New Testament gospels, including John. Chapters 14 – 17 of his book deal with the fourth gospel – a total of 112 pages. Bauckham begins with John 21:24–25:

> *This is the disciple who testifies of these things, and wrote these things; and we know that his testimony is true. And there are also many other things that Jesus did, which if they were written one by one, I suppose that even the world itself could not contain the books that would be written. Amen.*

These words point to the author. The author is the beloved disciple because the narrator says explicitly that the beloved disciple 'wrote these things'. The mention of 'these things' covers the whole gospel story, not just the events of John 21. In addition, the word 'wrote' is probably not causative: in other words, it does not mean that the beloved disciple caused someone else to write these things. Rather, it means that the beloved disciple wrote them himself. The beloved disciple is accordingly the author of the gospel of John. Even if the verb *graphein* (to write) is causative, at the very least this means that the beloved disciple dictated what we find in the gospel. As Bauckham says, 'John 21:24 means that the Beloved Disciple composed the Gospel, whether or not he wielded the pen.'[22] He was substantially responsible for the content of the story.

As for the beloved disciple himself, he is portrayed as a person in direct contact with Jesus and as someone who heard and saw Jesus at the critical moments of his life, especially during the last week of his ministry. He is most likely not John the son of Zebedee. Most scholars of the fourth gospel now regard the ancient association of the beloved disciple with this John to be wrong. There are simply too many arguments going against this theory for it to hold water. Today, the majority of scholars believe that the beloved disciple was a disciple of Jesus based in the Jerusalem area. So much of John's story takes place in and around Jerusalem, whereas in the other New Testament gospels the action takes place principally in Galilee (until of course the time of Jesus' passion). This is very hard to square with the traditional notion of the beloved disciple being John son of Zebedee, since this John came from the north, from Galilee, not from the south in Judea.

So the beloved disciple was a Jerusalem-based disciple. He was not one of the Twelve. The Twelve are not listed by name in John's gospel and the phrase 'the disciples' is preferred to the phrase 'the Twelve', which is only mentioned four times (Jn. 6:67, 6:70, 6:71; 20:24). The beloved disciple was accordingly not a well known disciple, certainly not as well known as Peter. At the same time, this anonymous disciple was an eyewitness of what occurred in Jesus' ministry in and around Jerusalem. While his testimony is less well known than Peter's, it still has a claim to validity alongside that of Peter. Indeed, it is even hinted that this eyewitness account has a greater sense of perception about Jesus than Peter's, hence the competitive note that attends the descriptions of the pairing of the beloved disciple and Peter.

It is important at this point to realise that there were two Johns mentioned by the earliest church theologians and historians. There was John the son of Zebedee and another John called 'John the Elder'. Richard Bauckham argues strongly that the gospel was named 'the Gospel According to John' by the second century AD, and that the John referred to was never John, Zebedee's son, but rather John the Elder, who was called 'Elder' because he lived to a very great age. This great age incidentally explains why there is a discussion concerning whether the beloved disciple will in fact die before Jesus returns (Jn. 21:23). Bauckham proposes that 'Old Man John' was in fact the beloved disciple and that this John not only authored the fourth gospel but also the three New Testament letters of John. The reason why he was known by the epithet 'the disciple whom Jesus loved' is that the leaders of the community of the fourth gospel knew the author of this story was not one of the Twelve. Far from trying to boost their credentials by plundering one of the names of the Twelve, they believed that anonymity had greater integrity than using a false name. As Bauckham compellingly argues, this is a major factor in favour of the historical credibility of this long-lived disciple of Jesus and his eyewitness testimony.

## Was John a High Priest?

Can we say anything more about this John the Elder? Bauckham goes on to say a great deal. The most intriguing question he asks is, 'Was this John a Jewish high priest?' Bauckham quotes Bishop Polycrates of Ephesus (c. AD 130–196) – the city where John's gospel is said to have been published. Eusebius the church historian (c. AD 275–339) records Polycrates saying the following in his *Church History* (chapter 24 of Book V):

> In Asia also great lights have fallen asleep, which shall rise again on the day of the Lord's coming,

when he shall come with glory from heaven, and shall seek out all the saints. Among these are Philip, one of the twelve apostles, who fell asleep in Hierapolis; and his two aged virgin daughters, and another daughter, who lived in the Holy Spirit and now rests at Ephesus; and, moreover, John, who was both a witness and a teacher, who reclined upon the bosom of the Lord, and, being a priest, wore the sacerdotal plate. He fell asleep at Ephesus.

Notice the reference to John wearing what Polycrates calls 'the sacerdotal plate'. What did he mean by that?

There has been much debate about this, but the simplest translation of the word *petalon* is 'the high priestly frontlet'. It refers to the headdress worn by the high priest in the Tabernacle and later in the Temple in Jerusalem. This was a blue linen head garment worn over the white turban. On it were inscribed the four letters of the sacred name for God, YHWH, known as the Tetragrammaton. This reference indicates that John the Elder (the John to whom Polycrates is referring) was a high priest who ministered in the Temple in Jerusalem, in succession to the original high priesthood of Aaron in the days of the Tabernacle.

How are we to interpret this? There are essentially two ways. The first is literally. Bauckham believes that Polycrates viewed John as a high priest in Jerusalem who became a follower of Jesus. He does not propose that Polycrates arrived at this position from historical research. Rather, he suggests that Polycrates read about the John in Acts 4:5–6 and supposed this to be the same John who is associated with the fourth gospel:

*And it came to pass, on the next day, that their rulers, elders, and scribes, as well as Annas the high priest,*

*Caiaphas, John, and Alexander, and as many as were of
the family of the high priest, were gathered together at
Jerusalem.*

The John mentioned here was a high priest – or at least of
the high priest's family – and corresponds to the high
priest mentioned by Josephus in Antiquities 18:123, who
is called Theophilus, son of Annas. Theophilus is the
Greek equivalent of Yohanan, or John. In the boldest
version of this theory John the author of the fourth gospel
is regarded as the high priest in Jerusalem known as John
but referred to by Josephus by the Greek name
Theophilus, who exercised his office from AD 37 to 41.
However, this version of the theory is dismissed by many
as implausible. Bauckham's view is that Polycrates
identified the Old Man John who died in Ephesus with
the high priest John mentioned in Acts 4:6, but he did so
purely on the basis of the texts of John and Acts, not on
the basis of historical information.

The second way in which this description has been
interpreted is metaphorically. In this version 'the
sacerdotal plate' is regarded as a metaphor for John the
Elder's spiritual authority. In other words, it is a symbol
for the fact that John was the equivalent of the Jewish
high priest. In the earliest church, Christian prophets
were referred to on at least one occasion as 'high priests'.
In the *Didache*, meaning 'Teaching' (a first-century
collection of Christian teachings dating from between AD
100 and 120), we read the following in 13:3–4:

Every firstfruit then of the produce of the wine-vat
and of the threshing-floor, of thy oxen and of thy
sheep, thou shalt take and give as the firstfruit to the
prophets; for they are your chief-priests.

It is possible that Polycrates' use of the image of 'the sacerdotal plate' was a metaphor for the fact that John the Elder was a prophetic leader in the church.

In the light of this, let me say that there are strong reasons for believing that the beloved disciple was very possibly a priest familiar with the Temple ministries. As long ago as 1922, C.F. Burney listed the reasons why the author of John's gospel had priestly connections. In his influential study *The Aramaic Origin of the Fourth Gospel*, Burney listed the following indications:

- The beloved disciple was well known to the high priest in Jerusalem and gained ready access to his house (Jn. 18:15–18)
- This gospel alone mentions the name of the high priest's servant, Malchus, whose ear Peter cuts off (Jn. 18:10)
- Only John's gospel tells us that one of those who questioned Peter was a relation of Malchus (18:26)
- This gospel shows special knowledge of Joseph of Arimathea and Nicodemus, who were members of the Sanhedrin
- This gospel has inside information of what happened at some of the meetings of the Sanhedrin (7:15–52, 11:47–53; 12:10)
- The fact that the beloved disciple took the mother of Jesus to his own home suggests that he had a residence in Jerusalem (19:27)[23]

Alongside these features we should add some observations taken from Martin Hengel's book *The Johannine Question*. His research has provided the following information:

First, John was a very popular name during the first century, especially in priestly circles. In fact, it was the

most common name for the high priest between the time
of Alexander the Great and Antiochus Epiphanes IV.
Yohanan and Eleazar were the two most frequent names
for priests in Jewish antiquity.

Secondly, the author of this gospel is very familiar with
the Jewish festivals, giving us accurate details about
Passover, Tabernacles and Hanukkah in particular.

Thirdly, the author is extremely well informed about
the topographical details in and around Jerusalem.

Fourthly, the author is aware of rituals and regulations
– for example, that the command to circumcise breaks the
Sabbath (7:22) and that stone vessels were used for
purification (2:6).

Fifthly, the gospel was written in Aramaic originally, or
a very Hebraic type of Greek. Thus we find transliterated
Aramaic words (1:38, 41, 42; 4:25; 9:7; 20:16). There are
other notable grammatical constructions that are telltale
signs of a person with a Hebraic mindset (such as
beginning sentences with a verb, a standard feature of
Hebrew/Aramaic). These linguistic data suggest that the
author's mother tongue was not Greek.

Finally, there are numerous similarities between the
imagery in John's gospel and that used throughout the
Qumran scrolls, especially the dualism of light and
darkness. Much of the thematic language of John – which
used to be regarded as Greek in character – is now seen as
thoroughly Jewish, in the light of the discovery of the
Dead Sea Scrolls.[24]

All these factors, in my opinion, point to the strong
possibility that the author of the fourth gospel, the
beloved disciple, was a priest. It is unlikely in my view
that John was the high priest in Jerusalem. At the same
time we know that the beloved disciple was *gnostos*, well
known, to the high priest at the time (Jn. 18:15). In other
words, the beloved disciple was on friendly terms with

the household of Annas and Caiaphas. This further confirms the likelihood that John was a priest who came to believe in Jesus. This sort of transformation did occur to Jewish priests, especially after Pentecost. For example, Acts 6:7 says that a great number of Jewish priests became obedient to Jesus. John may well have been a pre-Pentecost forerunner of these priests.

Putting all this together, it seems very possible to me that the author of the fourth gospel was the beloved disciple and that this person was a priest who ministered in the Jerusalem Temple and was on friendly terms with the high priest's household. This beloved disciple was called John and was an eyewitness of the ministry of Jesus in the Jerusalem and Judea area. He was not well known in comparison with the Twelve, so the gospel often presents him in a very positive light when he is seen in the same contexts as Simon Peter. This helps to boost his credibility and standing. This is further strengthened by the narrator's portrayal of the beloved disciple as a very perceptive witness. He sees what other disciples do not see and he sees with eagle-eyed precision. In other words, the beloved disciple remembers the details of events and penetrates to the spiritual significance within them. Above all, John is presented as an intimate friend of Jesus, one especially close to the Master's heart, with access to revelation that others did not have.

This John wore the 'sacerdotal plate' in the sense that he was chief among a group of prophetic leaders at the heart of the community for which the fourth gospel was written. This group is responsible for the claim, 'We know his testimony is true.' It is entirely possible that some of the priests who became followers of Jesus in Jerusalem formed part of this circle of people around John. It is also, in my view, likely that Mary Magdalene was one of the leaders in this group. I do not believe she

was the overall leader. Recent attempts to argue that
Mary Magdalene was in fact the beloved disciple are not
persuasive to me, because Mary Magdalene appears in at
least two scenes where the beloved disciple is also
present, and in addition the beloved disciple is always
referred to as male. Nevertheless, there is little doubt in
my mind that Mary Magdalene was an extremely
influential apostolic figure in the community over which
John the Elder presided. She is the 'apostle to the
apostles' in John 20:17–18 and was regarded at least in the
Eastern church as 'equal to the apostles'. Her prominence
in this community must not be downplayed – and nor
should John the Elder's.

## Four Mysterious Events

Yohanan the priest was the author responsible for the
encoded narrative in John 20:1–18. He saw that the grave
clothes, the angels and Mary Magdalene's encounter
with Jesus pointed to a great mystery. This mystery was
the revelation that the empty tomb had become like the
Holy of Holies. It was also that the risen Jesus had
secretly performed the role of the High Priest in the *Yom
Kippur* celebrations. He saw with keen insight that Mary
Magdalene had come upon Jesus as he was ascending to
his Father to present the sacrifice of his blood in the
throne room of heaven. He saw that Jesus had in fact
fulfilled the Day of Atonement, even as he had fulfilled
the Feasts of Passover and Tabernacles. He saw what the
writer to the Hebrews saw: 'Christ came as High Priest of
the good things to come, with the greater and more
perfect tabernacle not made with hands, that is, not of
this creation' (Heb. 9:11). This is the gospel secret that he
concealed within the events of the first Easter Day. Many

have passed over it. But those who have eyes to see can penetrate beneath the surface to the depths beneath. As many scholars have been fond of saying, John's gospel is indeed like a magic pool in which children can paddle and elephants can swim.

So there is a great mystery in John 20:1–18 – a Tabernacle revelation, a *Yom Kippur* secret. But the mystery does not end there. In the forty years after Jesus had died and then risen from the dead, we know that there were strange goings on in the Temple each year on the Day of Atonement. Four are worthy of mention.

The first we might call 'the miracle of the lot'.

If we recall the regulations for *Yom Kippur*, there were two goats chosen for sacrifice. One goat was chosen to be killed, and its blood was sprinkled on the mercy seat in the Holy of Holies. The other one was kept alive but sent out into the desert as a scapegoat. How was it decided which one would be killed and which one would be expelled? The answer is through the casting of lots. Two stones were used, a black stone and a white stone. In terms of probability, there was always an equal chance that the high priest would choose either. But for forty years in a row, from the time of Jesus' crucifixion onwards, the high priest always selected the black stone, never the white one. The chances of that happening are astronomical (two to the fortieth power). The black stone – for the goat killed as an offering to the Lord – was selected every time, a fact which caused consternation among the Jewish priests and signified to them that something fundamental had changed in the Day of Atonement ritual.

The second strange event we might call 'the miracle of the crimson cloth'. This has to do with the goat that was offered to the Lord as a sacrifice. The goat was tied by a crimson thread, and a strip of this cloth was tied to the

Temple door every year. It would turn white as a sign that the Lord found the sacrifice acceptable. This was connected with the promise in Isaiah 1:18:

> *Though your sins are like scarlet, they shall be as white as snow; though they are red like crimson, they shall be as wool.*

Every year until the death of Jesus (approximately AD 29), the crimson cloth was said to have turned white. However, every year after this – until AD 70, when the Temple was destroyed – the cloth remained crimson and would not turn white. The clear message was that the Day of Atonement was no longer acceptable to God. The sacrifice of the goat was no longer deemed effective for dealing with Israel's sins. The priests had always believed that the crimson cloth turning white was a sign that God approved of the Day of Atonement rituals. Now, as a result of Jesus' death on the Cross, *Yom Kippur* had become not only ineffective but obsolete.

The third strange event we might call 'the miracle of the open doors'. It is said by the rabbis that the doors of the Temple swung open of their own accord every night during *Yom Kippur* from AD 30 to 70. This frightened the Jewish leaders in Jerusalem and they could come up with no adequate explanation. Rabbi Yohannan Ben Zakkai declared

> O Temple, why do you frighten us? We know that you will end up destroyed. For it has been said, 'Open your doors, O Lebanon, that the fire may devour your cedars.' (Zechariah 11:1) (Sota 6:3)

The doors signified that something dramatic had changed as far as access to God's presence was concerned.

The final strange event we might call 'the miracle of the Temple menorah'.

For the forty years after Jesus' death the central lamp of the Temple menorah (the huge seven-branched lampstand) went out and would not shine. For 12,500 nights in a row the main lamp went out of its own accord no matter what precautions the priest tried to take. This lamp was not supposed to go out and was regarded as a kind of 'eternal flame'. Again, the odds against this happening are astronomical. Something supernatural was deemed to be at work. God was signifying that the light of his presence was now gone from the Temple. There simply is no other explanation.

How do we know all this? We find mention of these matters in both the Jerusalem and the Babylonian Talmud. These were books of Jewish history and commentary written in the centuries after the destruction of the Temple in AD 70 – i.e. the third to fifth centuries AD. Here's what the Jerusalem Talmud says:

> Forty years before the destruction of the Temple, the western light went out, the crimson thread remained crimson, and the lot for the Lord always came up in the left hand. They would close the gates of the Temple by night and get up in the morning and find them wide open.

A similar passage is found in the Babylonian Talmud:

> Our rabbis taught: During the last forty years before the destruction of the Temple the lot did not come up in the right hand; nor did the crimson coloured strap become white; nor did the western-most light shine; and the doors of the Hekel [Temple] would open by themselves.

Clearly there were mysterious happenings in the Temple at *Yom Kippur* between AD 30 and 70, between the death of Jesus and the destruction of the Temple. We know from Matthew's gospel that the veil that separated the Holy of Holies and the sanctuary had been torn from the top downwards at the moment of Jesus' death. In Matthew 27:50–51 we read

> *And Jesus cried out again with a loud voice, and yielded up His spirit. Then, behold, the veil of the temple was torn in two from top to bottom . . .*

This event – not to mention the four annual occurrences noted by the Talmudim – must have rocked the priests in Jerusalem. Little wonder, then, that Luke can report in Acts 6:7

> *Then the word of God spread, and the number of the disciples multiplied greatly in Jerusalem, and a great many of the priests were obedient to the faith.*

After Jesus' death and resurrection, a great number of priests were to follow suit after the outpouring of the Holy Spirit and the preaching of the gospel. John, the disciple whom Jesus had loved, had already come to see who Jesus was. Others followed afterwards.

How about you?

*God has raised this Jesus to life, and we are all witnesses of the fact.*

Acts 2:32 (NIV)

# Conclusion

Dan Brown's novel *The Da Vinci Code* was published by Doubleday in 2003. Since then it has become a bestseller in 150 countries. At the time of writing it has sold over forty million copies and been translated into forty-four languages. It is one of the most widely read books of our times.

And yet the novel has caused a great deal of controversy, not least because several of its lead characters make highly contentious claims about the most influential figure in human history, namely Jesus of Nazareth. In *The Da Vinci Code* it is proposed that the church has been engaged in a great cover-up since its beginnings two thousand years ago. This cover-up involves a secret so explosive it would rock the whole world on its axis were it to be discovered. Dan Brown believes he has decrypted the code.

So what is it? In a novel that is part conspiracy theory, part chase, part murder mystery, part pulp thriller, Dan Brown proposes that Jesus of Nazareth was in fact married to Mary Magdalene, that they had a child, and that their bloodline continues to this day. He argues that this secret was known by an ancient group called the Gnostics and that their accounts of Jesus – known as the 'Gnostic Gospels' – were destroyed by the early church.

He also claims that the facts were not completely destroyed and that a secret society known as the Priory of Sion continued to guard the hidden truth about Jesus.

One of the members of the Priory of Sion – according to Dan Brown – was Leonardo da Vinci. He knew that Jesus and Mary Magdalene had been married. So when he came to paint his picture of the Last Supper, he depicted a feminine-looking disciple next to Jesus – not John the Apostle, as in Christian tradition, but Mary Magdalene. Furthermore, the V-shape formed by the positions of Jesus and Mary Magdalene in the painting is symbolic of the cup that is absent from the table itself. The secret encoded within Leonardo's painting is this: the womb of Mary Magdalene is the Holy Grail.

While few deny Brown's skill in creating such suspenseful drama, few also deny that his views about Jesus, about Christianity and about the church are extremely controversial. Dan Brown claims at the beginning of his book that the novel is based on fact. In a TV interview he said all the history reported in the novel is factual. But is it?

My studies have revealed that the claim to factual accuracy made by Dan Brown is hard to sustain. In fact one non-Christian writer has recently done an exhaustive count of the factual errors in *The Da Vinci Code*. He found fifteen correct facts, seven partly correct facts and sixty-nine errors. Of these sixty-nine, eight are trivial. So that leaves sixty-one. But sixty-one means there's approximately one error for every seven-and-a-half pages!

Leonardo da Vinci once said that telling the truth is morally excellent. Superior intellects deal with the truth, he said, while wandering wits deal in falsehoods. Jesus was not married to Mary Magdalene, nor did he have a child, nor was this 'secret' covered up to make Jesus look more divine. From the very beginning Jesus was viewed as divine as well as human. So Brown's views are fiction, not fact (for more on this, see Appendix 1).

And facts are important! We live in a world where people are more and more constructing reality rather than discovering it. For example, James Cameron – the famous movie director responsible for the film *Titanic* – made a TV documentary called 'The Lost Tomb of Christ'. Cameron argued on this programme that ten ossuaries (small caskets used to store bones) contained the remains of Jesus and his immediate family, including Mary Magdalene. These ten ossuaries had been discovered when bulldozers flattened part of a Jerusalem suburb in 1980. One of the caskets had the inscription 'Judah, son of Jesus', which Cameron argued is evidence that Jesus had a son.

On the surface of it, a programme like this can sound convincing, especially to people who are completely unaware of the popularity of names like Jesus and Mary in the first century. But Dr Shimon Gibson – an archaeologist – summed up the prevailing scholarly view when he said at a press conference that he was very sceptical about Cameron's claims. Cameron himself has offered no actual proof and has admitted that the chances of these caskets containing Jesus' remains are 'a couple of million to one'. Amos Kloner, another archaeologist, said that the claims do not make for good archaeology but they do make for good TV. He reminded viewers in an interview that 'the names on the caskets are the most common names found among Jews at the time'.

In *The Resurrection Code* we have not been dealing with fiction but with facts. The story of the encounter between Mary Magdalene and the risen Jesus is not a fictional episode in the gospel. For all the artful re-description in this beautifully encoded text, there is a basis in fact in John 20:1–18. In the final verse of the Magdalene narrative, John 20:18, the narrator reports

*Mary Magdalene came and told the disciples that she had
seen the Lord, and that He had spoken these things to her.*

Here we are told that Mary communicated with the
disciples not only what she had seen but also what she
had heard – and indeed, we may presume, handled. Here
we are not that far from the kind of language used in
another document from John's orbit, the first letter of
John, chapter 1 verses 1–3:

*That which was from the beginning, which we have heard,
which we have seen with our eyes, which we have looked
upon, and our hands have handled, concerning the Word
of life – the life was manifested, and we have seen, and
bear witness, and declare to you that eternal life which
was with the Father and was manifested to us – that
which we have seen and heard we declare to you . . .*

The fact is, Mary Magdalene did exist and she did follow
Jesus throughout his ministry. She did witness Jesus'
death on the Cross and she was at the empty tomb on the
first Easter morning and met her resurrected Lord. All
these facts are attested to in the New Testament gospels
and even though there are differences in the details – the
grave clothes, the number of angels, and so forth – these
differences are actually compelling factors in favour of
the truthfulness of these accounts. Agreement on every
detail would cause us to suspect precisely the kind of
conspiracy that our culture loves so much today. But
there is an absence of that kind of contrived harmoni-
sation in these gospel accounts. We are dealing here with
history, not with myth.

And there are other factors that point in this direction
as well. I offer the following three comments in favour of
the historical reliability of the core events in John 20:1–18:

First, there is the priority of Mary Magdalene's testimony. Miriam of Magdala played a crucial part as an eyewitness of the resurrection of Jesus. We have already seen how John gives her the key role in this regard. Here is how Mark, Matthew and Luke begin their accounts of the empty tomb tradition:

- Mark 16:1 (NLT): *The next evening, when the Sabbath ended, Mary Magdalene and Salome and Mary the mother of James went out and purchased burial spices to put on Jesus' body.*
- Matthew 28:1 (NLT): *Early on Sunday morning, as the new day was dawning, Mary Magdalene and the other Mary went out to see the tomb.*
- Luke 24:1 (NLT): *But very early on Sunday morning the women came to the tomb, taking the spices they had prepared.*

Luke adds in verse 10 (NLT):

*The women who went to the tomb were Mary Magdalene, Joanna, Mary the mother of James, and several others.*

There is complete agreement about Mary Magdalene's leading role in the discovery of the empty tomb. Mary arrived at the tomb first, not the men. Furthermore, according to John's account, Mary was the first person to see the risen Lord as well. This is significant for two reasons. First of all, a woman's testimony was regarded as pretty well worthless in a court of law. Would John have put Mary Magdalene as the first witness to the empty tomb and the resurrection appearances if he was creating a plausible fiction? I think not. Second, the apostle Paul omits to mention the role of the women when he describes the resurrection in 1 Corinthians 15:3–5:

*For I delivered to you first of all that which I also received: that Christ died for our sins according to the Scriptures, and that He was buried, and that He rose again the third day according to the Scriptures, and that He was seen by Cephas [i.e. Peter], then by the twelve.*

Where is the mention of Mary Magdalene in this list? For Paul, Mary Magdalene's presence as the first one to see the risen Jesus is not mentioned. This is not because it did not happen but precisely because it did happen! Paul leaves this memory out because he knows that it harms the credibility of the resurrection tradition in a male-dominated culture where a woman's report is regarded as an idle tale (see Luke 24:11). John, on the other hand, is unembarrassed by Mary Magdalene's part in the two traditions of the empty tomb and the appearances of the risen Lord. There is a strong argument here for believing that John has based his account on facts, not fiction. Why would someone, especially a Jewish Christian writing to a predominantly Jewish audience, create a version where a woman is the primary witness? In that culture it would lack credibility. But it is precisely the unabashed inclusion and prioritisation of Mary Magdalene which makes this account what C.H. Dodd called the most self-authenticating of all the resurrection narratives.

A second factor that needs to be considered is what we might call the restraint of the author. John 20:1–18 is told with zero hype. What is noticeable about this narrative right from its opening words is the lack of dramatic embellishment and intrusive explanation. Instead, there is brevity about the way this story is narrated and there are, as I have pointed out all along, many gaps in the storytelling. And the biggest gap of all is any description of Jesus actually rising from the tomb. In John's story we go straight from the burial at the end of John 19 to the empty tomb in John 20. But how did the tomb become empty? Who rolled the stone away? What happened to Jesus' body in the grave clothes? Where did Jesus go?

John's account stops short of filling in these kinds of gaps. The reason is quite simple: no human witness saw the sacred moments in which Jesus' dead body was transformed by the divine glory into a resurrected, spiritual body. No human witness saw the stone being supernaturally rolled away from the entrance of the tomb. How different from the unrestrained, imaginative speculations of fictional writers! This is the very opposite of fictional composition, where the author can describe what he likes and invent what he wants. And this is where John differs so markedly from later fictional, Gnostic or 'secret' gospels. The second-century Gospel of Peter is in fact a great example. There is no restraint in this gospel's narration of the moment of Christ's resurrection!

Now in the night whereon the Lord's day dawned, as the soldiers were keeping guard two by two in every watch, there came a great sound in the heaven, and they saw the heavens opened and two men descend thence, shining with a great light, and drawing near unto the sepulchre. And that stone which had been set on the door rolled away of itself and went back to the side, and the sepulchre was opened and both of the young men entered in. When therefore those soldiers saw that, they waked up the centurion and the elders (for they also were there keeping watch); and while they were yet telling them the things which they had seen, they saw again three men come out of the sepulchre, and two of them sustaining the other, and a cross following, after them. And of the two they saw that

their heads reached unto heaven, but of him that
was led by them that it overpassed the heavens. And
they heard a voice out of the heavens saying: Hast
thou (or Thou hast) preached unto them that sleep?
And an answer was heard from the cross, saying:
Yea.

This account of the resurrection is manifestly different
from the one we find in John's gospel. In the Gospel of
Peter we have a loud sound from heaven, angels
descending from heaven in a bright light, the stone
rolling away all on its own, three figures up to sixty
thousand feet tall, and most silly of all, a walking and
talking Cross! John's account contains nothing like this. It
does not describe the actual moment of resurrection but
begins with Mary Magdalene coming to the tomb after
the event. Thereafter the tale is told with great economy –
an economy which is partly created by the use of
'gaps'. We can conclude from all this that the author was
not composing a great fiction designed to manipulate
people into joining a movement but was rather relating
facts.

A third factor in favour of John's historicity here is
what I call the importance of the first day. The opening
words of John 20 highlight the significance of the first day
of the week:

*On the first day of the week Mary Magdalene went to the
tomb early, while it was still dark, and saw that the stone
had been taken away from the tomb.*

Later on in the same chapter, the narrator again uses the
phrase 'the first day' in his description of the appearance
of the risen Jesus to his disciples. John 20:19 tells us

> *Then, the same day at evening, being the first day of the*
> *week, when the doors were shut where the disciples were*
> *assembled, for fear of the Jews, Jesus came and stood in the*
> *midst, and said to them, 'Peace be with you.'*

Notice here the strong emphasis on 'the first day of the week'. Why does the narrator stress this point?

The first day of the week refers to what we today call Sunday. The seventh day of the Jewish week is the Sabbath, stretching from Friday 6pm to Saturday 6pm. Sabbath, or Shabbat, is a day of rest. It is the highlight, focus and completion of the week. The number seven is associated with perfection in Judaism and everything about this seventh day is regarded as perfect.

The first day of the week is the day after, running from Saturday 6pm to Sunday 6pm. In the Western world, most people regard the first day of the week as Monday. Time was calculated very differently in the New Testament era. This is why people often get confused about the references to Jesus rising on the third day. We must be careful not to fall into the trap of imposing our understanding of days on a Jewish Christian document of the first century. In the original context, Jesus would have died on the day that stretched from Thursday 6pm to Friday 6pm. That was day one. He would then have been in the tomb from Friday 6pm to Saturday 6pm. That was day two. On day three – Saturday 6pm to Sunday 6pm – he was resurrected. That was day three – the third day (for more on this, see Appendix 2).

Why is it so important that John stresses 'the first day of the week'? He is a Jewish Christian author writing for a Jewish audience. Something really momentous must have occurred for him, as a Jew, to redirect the spotlight away from the seventh day (Shabbat) to the first day of the week. As a Jewish follower of Jesus the author knew full well that Shabbat was the most holy day. To this day the following prayer is used on Friday evening:

> Blessed are You, Lord our God, King of the universe, who has hallowed us with His commandments, has desired us, and has given us, in love and goodwill, His holy Shabbat as a heritage, in remembrance of the work of Creation; the first of the holy festivals, commemorating the Exodus from Egypt. For You have chosen us and sanctified us from among all the nations, and with love and goodwill given us Your holy Shabbat as a heritage. Blessed are You Lord, who hallows the Shabbat.

In Jewish literature, poetry and music, Shabbat is described as a queen. In Talmudic literature we learn that Rabbi Hanina used to wrap himself in festive clothes toward evening on Friday and say, 'Come, let us go to receive Shabbat the Queen.' Likewise, Rabbi Yannai used to put on festive clothes on the eve of the Sabbath and say, 'Come, O bride, come O bride!' It is said, 'More than Israel has kept Shabbat, Shabbat has kept Israel.'

How come a Jewish writer in a Jewish Christian community has made the first day of the week the emphasis? We must come up with an explanation for this. The only answer is that a cataclysmic event has occurred that has caused him to see the first day of the week as the most important day of the week. To be sure, this author – because he was Jewish – would have continued to see the Sabbath as the Queen of Days. But now the first day of the week is the King of Days, because it causes him to remember that it was on this day that Jesus of Nazareth was raised from the dead. So right from the earliest days of the church, Jewish followers of Jesus are not only worshipping on the Sabbath, they are also gathering for a celebration of the resurrection early in the morning of the first day of the week (Acts 20:7). The account in John 20:1–18 reflects this practice and is compelling evidence for the world-changing events that led to this sea change in emphasis.

So three reasons from within John 20:1–18 itself indicate that we are dealing with facts, not fiction, in the report of the encounter between Mary Magdalene and Jesus at the empty tomb. Other factors could be included. For example, it is not likely that the earliest Christians would have invented a story about Jesus appearing first to a woman with the kind of past described in Luke 8:2. Nor is it likely that they would have included Mary Magdalene's lament about people having removed Jesus' body from the tomb, with the suggestion of grave robbery (surely playing into the hands of anyone wanting to make that charge). And it is highly unlikely that they would have created a story in which Mary Magdalene was given the responsibility of being the one to tell the disciples that Jesus was risen.

There are so many reasons why John 20:1–18 has what has been called 'the ring of truth' about it. As William Temple once wrote of this great narrative, 'It is most manifestly the record of a personal memory. Nothing else can account for the little details, so vivid, so little like the kind of thing that comes from invention or imagination.'[25] To be sure, John 20:1–18 is not a straight documentary account of events, devoid of theological intention or poetic retelling. It is what Franz Mussner called 'charismatic history'. It is the kind of historical narrative in which the significance of events – implicit within the events themselves – is made explicit. At the same time it is truth as well as beauty – truth beautifully and artfully recounted. Even Dan Brown has commented that there is something sacred about the resurrection. In a press statement in 2006 he said, 'The resurrection is perhaps the sole controversial Christian topic about which I would not desire to write; questioning the resurrection undermines the very heart of Christian belief.' To put it another way, Brown seems to be saying that the resurrection, for him, has *noli me tangere* written over it.

I hope that *The Resurrection Code* has revealed something of the riches within the New Testament gospels themselves. We do not really need to go chasing after secret gospels. There are gospel secrets yet to be fully disclosed. John 20:1–18 is ample evidence for this. There really is an Easter enigma here, one which is far more exciting than anything we might find in the current spate of code-breaker claims in the world of literature and art. In this encoded text we meet one who took on the role of the high priest, left his garments in the tomb as a sign, and offered his atoning sacrifice to the Father in heaven. This man's acts change everything. They change history, because history is never the same again. As H.G. Wells put it, 'I am an historian, I am not a believer, but I must confess as a historian that this penniless preacher from Nazareth is irrevocably the very centre of history. Jesus Christ is easily the most dominant figure in all history.' They change our lives too, if we allow them to. The entrance of the tomb remains open. Look in. What do you see? The ending of the story remains open. How will it end for you?

# Appendix 1

# Fact and Fiction in Dan Brown's *Da Vinci Code*

After the publication of Dan Brown's *The Da Vinci Code*, and in preparation for the release of the movie in May 2006, my wife and I decided we would create a scratch card to be distributed in all the multiplex cinemas in the country. This would have ten questions about the claims of *The Da Vinci Code* concerning Jesus, with fact or fiction options for answers. In conjunction with the Christian Enquiry Agency (CEA), we distributed 300,000 of these to the cinemas four weeks before the movie version was shown. In addition, we created a state-of-the-art web site with the answers to the questions, and a beautifully produced free booklet which could be either downloaded or sent for. In the weeks after the cinemas received these scratch cards, the newspapers and the TV reported on them in a major way. All the cards were taken by people enquiring about Jesus, and the CEA received thousands of phone calls from people seeking more information about the real Jesus. Many people who held wrong ideas about Jesus (or no ideas at all) were helped, and some reported that their lives had been changed through discovering what Mary Magdalene discovered – that Jesus is alive.

Here are ten claims made by characters in Dan Brown's novel and which formed the basis of the booklet and the web site:

## Claim 1

Mary Magdalene had a place of significance in the group that followed Jesus of Nazareth.
TRUE!
We know that Mary Magdalene was a follower of Jesus. According to Luke chapter 8, Jesus delivered her from seven evil spirits. Having been set free by Jesus, she chose to follow him with devotion. So she is present at the Cross when others flee. She is then the first to the empty tomb. When the risen Jesus meets Mary she seeks to embrace him. He asks her not to cling on to him and then asks her to tell the disciples that he is ascending to his Father.

Clearly Mary Magdalene was a woman of significance in the group that followed Jesus. Of the eight occasions when Mary Magdalene is mentioned in the gospels, her name is first in seven of the lists. The church has not always appreciated her primacy, though. As we have seen, in the sixth century AD, Pope Gregory linked her with the unnamed 'immoral woman' at the end of Luke chapter 7. This further damaged the honour of her name.

## Claim 2

The marriage of Jesus and Mary Magdalene is a matter of historical record.
FALSE!
This view is uttered by Sir Leigh Teabing on page 244

of *The Da Vinci Code*. It is in fact utterly without foundation. There is no single Christian document that suggests that Jesus and Mary Magdalene were married. With one voice, the four gospels in the New Testament clearly portray Jesus as a single, not a married, man. Not even the secret or 'Gnostic Gospels' (which Dan Brown mentions he relies on a lot) say that Jesus and Mary Magdalene were married.

Dan Brown brings in other arguments. For example, he claims that Jewish men were expected to be married. But in Jesus' day the expectations were far more flexible. John the Baptist (the Jewish prophet who heralded Jesus' coming) was single. The Jewish apostle Paul was unmarried and encouraged single people to remain that way (1 Cor. 7:8). And Jesus himself approved of singleness as a counter-cultural lifestyle (Mt. 19:10–12).

## Claim 3

The church knew from the earliest days that Jesus and Mary Magdalene had had a child.

FALSE!

On page 255 of *The Da Vinci Code* it is claimed that Mary Magdalene was pregnant at the time of Jesus' crucifixion and that Jesus was the father. With the help of Joseph of Arimathea (in whose tomb Jesus was buried), Mary Magdalene travelled to France secretly and took refuge in a Jewish community. There she gave birth to a baby daughter who was given the name Sarah. From Sarah's offspring comes the secret bloodline of Christ.

All this is factually inaccurate. The whole story is in fact a legend that started eight hundred years after Jesus. In a recent prime-time documentary on *The Da Vinci Code*, Elizabeth Vargas' conclusion was this: 'We found that there was no evidence of a child of Jesus and Mary Magdalene.' 'We didn't find any proof,' she added. And that is simply because there isn't any to be found! Even the most sceptical scholars admit that Jesus of Nazareth was not married and had no children.

**Claim 4**

Other 'gospels' (accounts of Jesus' life) besides those in the New Testament have been discovered in Egypt.
TRUE!
In 1945, a young Arab boy called Muhammad Ali Al-Samman made one of the greatest archaeological discoveries when he unearthed fifty texts in a field near Nag Hammadi in Upper Egypt. These texts contained a number of scriptures belonging to a diverse group called the Gnostics (who believed that human beings can experience salvation through *gnosis* or 'knowledge'). Among these scriptures were the Gospel of Philip, the Gospel of Truth and the Gospel of Thomas.

Dan Brown rightly notes that the Gnostic gospels provide a very different picture of Jesus from that found in the New Testament gospels (page 234). However, he is wrong to say that they present the oldest records about Jesus. The Nag Hammadi gospels date from about AD 250–350. They are based on Greek texts from the early third century. So they are not as old as the New Testament gospels, nor are they based on eyewitness testimony. And there were not eighty of them as Brown claims (more like eleven).

## Claim 5

The 'secret' Gospel of Philip tells us that Mary Magdalene often kissed Jesus on the mouth.

FALSE!

One of the alternative gospels discovered at the Nag Hammadi library was the Gospel of Philip. This is not based on an eyewitness who knew Jesus. Even liberal scholars agree it is a late third-century document. In spite of this fact, Dan Brown makes much of it as an historical source (page 246), pointing to the saying that Mary Magdalene was the 'companion' of Jesus and that he 'loved her more than all the disciples and used to kiss her often on the mouth'.

It is really important to know that the original manuscript does not contain the word 'mouth'. There is a tantalising 'blank' at this point in the manuscript. Dan Brown says it reads 'mouth' but it doesn't! It could have read head, hand, cheek or anything. So he is wrong to make too much of this. And he is also wrong to say that 'companion' means 'spouse' in Aramaic. The saying is in any case in Coptic, not Aramaic. So his views here are full of basic errors.

## Claim 6

The Roman Emperor Constantine (AD 274–337) was responsible for deciding the Bible as we know it today.

FALSE!

Constantine was proclaimed emperor in AD 306. The church historian Eusebius claims Constantine had a vision of the Cross and converted to Christianity. Seeing the Cross, Constantine is said to have also seen the inscription, 'In this sign you will conquer.' In AD 313 he issued the Edict of Milan, which recognised Christianity as an official religion throughout the Roman Empire. It also granted Christians the freedom to worship and reparation for all losses under persecution.

Brown is right to identify the importance of Constantine but he is wrong to say that the emperor decided which documents went into the New Testament (page 231). The process for that had begun 150 years before Constantine and concluded after Constantine had died, in AD 367, when Bishop Athanasius proclaimed the twenty-seven books of the New Testament agreed on by all Christians. Even the four gospels of Matthew, Mark, Luke and John were referred to as the 'fourfold' gospel from the earliest times.

## Claim 7

The bishops of the early church met at the Council of Nicaea in AD 325 to discuss Jesus' divinity.

TRUE!

There had been debates about Jesus in the church from about the mid-second century AD. However, a major difference of opinion flared up because an elderly priest called Arius argued that Jesus was not a divine being like God the Father but a being created by the Father before the world began. The Emperor Constantine saw it as his responsibility to put an end to the quarrels about this and he called all 318 of the bishops to a council in Nicaea (modern Iznik in Turkey) in AD 325.

Dan Brown is right to say that the council met to talk about the divinity of Christ. But he is wrong when he says that the bishops voted on whether Jesus was divine and that the vote was only just carried. The fact is the bishops met to discuss whether Arius' views were right or not, and they voted that they were not, 316 saying Arius was wrong and only two that he was right. The council then formulated the Nicene Creed, which is still recited by Christians today.

## Claim 8

Prior to the Council of Nicaea, the church believed that Jesus of Nazareth was just a mortal prophet.

FALSE!

Dan Brown makes this claim on page 233 of *The Da Vinci Code*. But this is the very opposite of the truth. Five hundred verses of the New Testament actually pre-suppose that Jesus was more than just a human being, that he was both God and Man. Thomas, who was said to doubt Jesus' resurrection, eventually came to confess Jesus as 'my Lord and my God' (John's Gospel chapter 20 verse 28). Jesus is described as having divine attributes in many places in the New Testament.

After the New Testament era (AD 30–100), the following centuries witnessed continued confessions of the divinity of Jesus. In AD 150 Justin Martyr said that Jesus is 'even God'. In AD 185, Irenaeus proclaimed that Jesus is 'our Lord and God and Saviour and King'. Clement of Alexandria in about AD 200 said that Jesus was 'truly most manifest Deity . . . equal to the Lord of the Universe'. The divinity of Jesus was therefore not an idea invented in AD 325 at Nicaea.

## Claim 9

Leonardo da Vinci was a member of the Priory of Sion, a secret society which knew about Jesus' child.

FALSE!

There was indeed a Priory of Sion in the Middle Ages but this is not the one to which Dan Brown refers. Dan Brown is talking about the secret society concocted by a Frenchman called Pierre Plantard. Plantard created a series of forged documents in the 1960s and 1970s, designed to prove the existence of a bloodline from Jesus and Mary through the kings of France to himself (claiming in the process to be the rightful heir to the throne!).

Plantard and his associates referred to themselves as the Priory of Sion and placed the 'secret records' in libraries all over France. In 1993, however, Plantard admitted under oath to a French judge that he had invented these documents about the Priory of Sion. He was given a stern caution and dismissed as a crank. Dan Brown's view that Leonardo da Vinci was a member of this alleged Priory is based on one of Plantard's forged documents.

## Claim 10

Art historians agree that Leonardo's painting 'The Last Supper' shows Mary Magdalene next to Jesus.

FALSE!

In *The Da Vinci Code* it is argued that Leonardo da Vinci was a member of the Priory of Sion, a secret society that knew about Jesus' marriage to Mary Magdalene. Leonardo divulges the secret in an encoded way in his painting 'The Last Supper'. There he depicts a female figure sitting at Jesus' right hand at the last meal Jesus shared with his disciples. This is not John the son of Zebedee (as in traditional paintings of the Last Supper) but Mary Magdalene.

The fact is that art historians have long recognised the individual in question as the young apostle John. Noted Princeton professor of art history Dr Jack Wasserman says that artists in Florence (where Leonardo lived at the time) commonly painted John the apostle as a young, somewhat feminine-looking male. Leonardo painted other male Bible characters in a very feminine way, including John the Baptist. Dan Brown's view therefore does not reflect the mainstream view of art historians.

# Appendix 2

# He Arose! . . . But When?

*Dwight A. Pryor*

Jesus of Nazareth offered up himself as a sacrifice on behalf of humanity during the Festival of Redemption, Passover. He quickly was placed into a borrowed tomb nearby because the Sabbath was approaching. On the third day, God caused him to live again by the power of the Holy Spirit. This is the consistent witness of all the apostles.

The evidence for the resurrection is compelling, both in the multiplicity of witnesses and in the transformation of the dispirited disciples left in disarray by his shocking death. A 'crucified Messiah' was a theological contradiction in their worldview. *That* he arose seems abundantly clear. What is less certain is the timing. *When* did Jesus actually come forth from the grave?

Church tradition has long celebrated the resurrection at dawn on Easter morning. All four gospels indeed attest that it occurred on Sunday, the first day of the week. But was it at sunrise? Matthew's gospel provides an interpretative key that suggests otherwise.

The Greek of Matthew 28:1 preserves ancient Hebrew terminology: *'Late of the Sabbath in the dawning (lighting)*

150

*toward the first day of the week.'* This awkward Greek construction points to the common Hebrew idiom, *motza'ei Shabbat* or the 'going out' of the Sabbath – i.e., the transition between the end of the Sabbath and the 'dawning' or beginning of the next day.

Remember that in the Bible a day is reckoned from sunset to sunset ('It was evening and it was morning . . .'). The Sabbath is kept from 'evening unto evening' (Lev. 23:32), and thus the first day of the week actually begins just after sunset on what we call Saturday evening, using a Roman frame of reference.

What Matthew is suggesting therefore is that Jesus arose not at dawn on Sunday morning but shortly after the Sabbath ended – on Saturday evening!

Does this make sense in view of other facts recorded in the gospels? John 20:1ff is the most detailed literary account of the events surrounding the resurrection. Using it as a guide, consider the following:

- John notes that it was dark when Mary Magdalene went to the tomb on the first day of the week (20:1).
- If the Sabbath ended around 6:00 p.m. why would Mary, in her great devotion (and according to Luke, her desire to properly prepare the Lord's body for burial) wait another twelve hours before going to the nearby tomb? Why not go at the first available opportunity? If she was prepared to go in the dark of the early morning hours, how much more the preceding evening?
- Mary reports the news of an empty tomb to the apostles, who investigate (20:2–10). Following their departure she encounters the risen Messiah in the garden, who sends her to announce: 'I have seen the Lord!' (20:18).
- In the next verse Jesus shows himself to the disciples

who have assembled in a home. John specifies that this occurred '*on the evening of that day, the first day of the week*' (20:19).

- If the resurrection occurred at sunrise on Sunday morning, as we assume, then in biblical reckoning the evening later that day would not have been Sunday but the start of the *second* day of the week, Monday.
- For Jesus to appear to his disciples on the evening of the first day of the week, as John reports, he had to arise *earlier* on that same evening!
- Had he arisen at dawn and waited more than twelve hours later, after sunset, to meet with his disciples, it would have been the next day and not 'the first day of the week'.
- A more plausible explanation surely is that soon after his encounter with Mary Magdalene, Yeshua appeared to the apostles also, and all this transpired during *motza'ei Shabbat*. John's record of events is consistent with Matthew's Hebrew idiom.

Jesus did arise from the grave at the 'dawning' of Sunday – but in the Jewish frame of reference, not the Roman one. Thereafter, following their normal Sabbath synagogue participation, believers in the Messiah would continue to meet from house to house on *motza'ei Shabbat* (cf. Acts 20:7; 1 Cor. 16:2). They assembled on the evening of the first day of the week, remembering the risen Lord.

# Notes

1. Brown, R.E., *The Gospel According to John*, Volume 1 (New York: Doubleday, 1966), lxxxvii
2. Schneiders, S., 'Women in the Fourth Gospel' in Mark Stibbe (ed.), *The Gospel of John as Literature* (Leiden: E.J. Brill, 1993), 130
3. Schneiders, S., *ibid*, 141
4. Schneiders, S., *ibid*, 142
5. Jenkins, P., 'The Greatest Exaggerations Ever Told: a Critique of the "New" Interpretations of the Gnostic Gospels' in Dan Burstein and Arne de Keijzer (eds.), *Secrets of Mary Magdalene: The Untold Story of History's Most Misunderstood Woman* (Orion: London, 2006), 119
6. Jenkins, P., *ibid*, 121
7. See Lincoln, A.T., *The Gospel According to St John* (Peabody: Hendrickson, 2005), 495–496
8. Crossan, J.D., *Jesus: A Revolutionary Biography* (San Francisco: Harper, 1995), 157
9. Thiessen, K., 'Jesus and Women in the Gospel of John', *Direction* 19 (1990) 2.52–64 (for web version see http://www.directionjournal.org/article/?680)
10. Iser, W., 'The Reading Process: a Phenomenological Approach' in David Lodge (ed.), *Modern Criticism and Thought: A Reader* (London: Longman, 1988), 216

11. Richmond, B., *Jewish Insights into the New Testament* (Florida: Thunderbird Books, 1996), 43–46
12. Westcott, B.F., *The Gospel According to St. John* (London: 1880), 291
13. Temple, W., *Readings in St John's Gospel* (London: Macmillan, 1950), 361
14. Brown, R.E., *Gospel According to John*, Volume 2 (1970), 989
15. Lincoln, A.T., *Gospel According to St. John*, 492
16. Dodd, C.H., *Historical Tradition in the Fourth Gospel* (Cambridge: Cambridge University Press, 1963), 148
17. D'Angelo, M.R., 'A Critical Note: John 20:17 and the Apocalypse of Moses 31', *Journal of Theological Studies* 41 (1990), 531
18. Hoskyns, E.C., *The Fourth Gospel* (London: Faber, 1954), 542–543
19. Brown, R.E., *Gospel According to John*, Volume 1 (1966), 132
20. Tovey, D., *Narrative Art and Act in the Fourth Gospel* (Sheffield: Sheffield Academic Press, 1997), 140
21. Bauckham, R., *Jesus and the Eyewitnesses. The Gospels as Eyewitness Testimony* (Grand Rapids: Eerdmans, 2006), 399
22. Bauckham, R., *ibid*, 362
23. Burney, C.F., *The Aramaic Origin of the Fourth Gospel* (Oxford: Clarendon Press, 1922)
24. Hengel, M., *The Johannine Question*, tr. John Bowden (London: SCM, 1990), 109–111
25. Temple, W., *Readings in St John's Gospel* (London: Macmillan, 1950), 358